ANSWERS TO LIFE'S TOUGHEST QUESTIONS

RAYMOND C. HUNDLEY

Blessings!

Dr. Ray

To our children—Joel, Jon, Shelley and Brittany—who have asked me more questions than I could ever answer and have challenged me to go deeper in the answers I have given them. They have often answered my questions with thoughts I had never even considered. I love them for that and for never letting me off the hook when I went the wrong way.

Contents

Acknowledgments

I want to express special thanks to my good friend Bruce Ryskamp, former president and CEO of Zondervan Publishing House. Bruce read every page of this book, critiqued each chapter and offered invaluable suggestions for improving it. He also championed the book among many of his colleagues and friends in the publishing industry. I cannot thank him enough for his support of and contribution to this work.

I also want to give a word of appreciation to the Rev. Joshua Keith, the youth pastor of our church. He agreed to read the manuscript, offer comments and recommendations, and dialogue with me about its more controversial subjects. His editing and commentary made this a much better book, and I am thankful to him for his dedication to that process and for his friendship.

My college teaching colleague Myra Jones was instrumental in revamping the structure of this book. Her comments and advice helped shape its final form, and her interaction with me about its content (Myra is an atheist) sharpened its message for those who do not share the Christian faith. Above all, Myra is not just a critic but a dear friend as well.

Finally, and most significantly, I want to express my gratitude to my wife, Sharyn, who painstakingly edited every word in the manuscript, advised me about numerous aspects of it and constantly encouraged me to begin this project and to finish it. She is God's great treasure to me and I thank him constantly for giving her to me as my best friend, ideal soul mate, loving wife and best counselor. I could not carry out this writing ministry without her support for and commitment to me.

Introduction

Questions, questions, questions! It all began for me when my wife and I were invited to speak at the University of Iowa. We entered the room and there were more than four hundred university students staring at us. I had prayed about what to say to them, but all of a sudden I went blank. I definitely felt the Lord leading me to let them ask questions, and try to answer them from his Word. So I did. What was supposed to be a one-hour session stretched to two hours as they asked question after question and the Lord helped me answer them in ways most of them had never heard before. One graduate student in particular was very belligerent in the beginning of the session, but he came up to me afterward and said, "I want you to know you have really given me something to think about. I've never heard anyone explain the Christian faith the way you do." Well, that did it. I was hooked on the idea of doing question-and-answer sessions whenever possible so that I could deal with the questions people actually struggled with instead of trying to guess what they needed to hear. Since then we have seen thousands of Christians strengthened in their faith and hundreds of people come to faith in Christ as a result of those Q&A sessions.

Everywhere I go people have questions. The funny thing is—they are often the same ones. I have done Q&As in the United States, Latin America, Europe, Asia and Africa, and there seems to be a common set of questions all over the world. I love answering questions, or at least trying to answer them. After more than forty-five years of answering questions in churches, youth groups, universities, high schools, seminaries and Bible schools, I have learned much from my questioners. Many times over the years I have not known how to answer a question, but I have studied and talked with experts and found the answer for the next time it comes up. I really believe that it is far better to "scratch where people itch" than to throw out my ideas about what I think they need to hear.

As a result, over the years I have amassed a list of most-asked, tough questions, and I have spent a great deal of my time and study trying to answer them. Whether speaking to committed Christians or confirmed atheists, I have tried to respect everyone's questions and give the most objective, clear and honest answers I can give. But one of the frustrations has been that sometimes people want a two-minute answer to a two-hour question. That is, some questions are much more involved and complicated than others, and it takes quite a while to answer them fully and fairly. Generally, in public Q&As, I do not have enough time to do that. So I wrote this book using those often-repeated questions and answering them more fully than I can in a public forum. That is what this book is all about—answering those questions.

Let me be perfectly clear about one thing: I am offering *my answers* in this book, not *the answers*. I have seen my answers change enough over the years to realize that I don't have the final word on anything. The answers you are about to read are the result of my wrestling with some difficult, extremely significant questions over decades. I may well have more light on all of them in the future, but for right now, this is where I am on these issues; and I am open to correction and refutation.

Perhaps that's the ultimate value of a book like this one: not that you will swallow every answer I give, but that my answers will rouse you to come up with your own answers. So, I invite you to journey with me through some of the toughest questions I have ever been asked, and think through the answers I present as a springboard to your own study, wrestling and reflection on these very important issues. Your corrections, improvements, affirmations, criticisms and, yes, your *questions* will be greatly appreciated. You can contact me on my website: *AskDoctorRay.net*. I await your response. God bless you as you read.

PART ONE

Questions About
the Bible

Most people have two main questions about the Bible: How do you know it is from God, and can we trust what it says? With so many faiths and their Scriptures being presented to us these days, many people no longer believe that the Bible is a unique book. They believe it is just like all the other religions' texts: interesting moral teachings invented by people who wanted to make others behave themselves, and fascinating myths or legends that never really happened but are used to illustrate those moral standards.

Christianity's claim that the Bible is the only true revelation from God and that what it records really did happen in time and space flies in the face of much modern thought. But what if it is true? What if the Bible really is revealed by God? What if its message actually comes from him? What if the amazing things it presents really did happen just as the writers said they did? If that is true, we are living in a very different world from the one many people imagine. We live in a world in which God himself has acted supernaturally in human history. We live in a world in which he has not only acted but has also revealed the meaning of his actions and their implications for our lives. We live in a world in which God is a personal, communicative being who created us, has a plan for how we can live the best possible life and has made that plan clear to us in his revealed Word.

So, let's look together at four ingredients in this concept of God revealing himself to humanity:

1. the inspired nature of Scripture as a revelation from God

2. the assumption that the Bible is not trustworthy and is full of contradictions

3. the criteria that were used to identify the books that were actually revealed by God and reject those that were not

4. the evidence in favor of the reality of the most incredible miracle in the Bible—the resurrection of Jesus Christ

If we can settle those issues, we can then move on to say what God has shared in his Word about the many problems, challenges and opportunities we all face. Confidence in the authority and truthfulness of the Bible is the bedrock foundation of everything else in the Christian life. If we trust God's Word, that trust will open up doors for us that lead to the amazing adventure of living in a world of faith, confidence and certainty that shows the world of doubt and unbelief to be like a person stumbling around in a blackout with a flashlight in hand that has no batteries in it—the right tool, but no light to see reality. If God has spoken and his Word is meant to be a light to show us what is true and how to live, we would be foolish to ignore its light and stay with battery-less flashlights. Let's see if the light comes on for you today!

1

Why Would Anyone Believe the Bible Is the Inspired Word of God?

In all of my question-and-answer sessions, I always stress that I am an evangelical Christian, and therefore I intend to make sure that all my answers come from God's Word, not my own thoughts. Inevitably, someone in the audience will ask, "OK, but how do you know the Bible is true? Why do you think it's the inspired Word of God?" This is the central question for Christian faith. Everything else we believe is based on this foundational belief in the inspiration and authority of God's Word. That belief is the foundation for this book too. As is often the case, the most important principles are often the most difficult ones to articulate. Just ask someone to define *faith* and see how they do. So let's look at this crucial question and see how Christians deal with it.

THE CUMULATIVE ARGUMENT

The kind of argument I want to present in this chapter was popularized by Basil Mitchell in his book *The Justification of Religious Belief*.[1] In this work he presents the idea of a "cumulative argument" for Christianity. He says that when you put together all of the arguments in favor of the Christian faith, they present an alternative to atheism that more logically and consistently explains the data of the universe than any system without God could ever do. That is the approach I will take about the question of the Bible as the inspired Word of God. I hope to show you that it is reasonable, logical and probable to conclude that the Bible is the inspired Word of God rather than mere human literature.

The idea of cumulative argument is like the construction of a house. Standing on their own, the windows, walls and doors will not sustain the house. But when they are put together and well-constructed, they form a house that can withstand a hurricane. None of the eight arguments I will present can stand on their own as proof of the inspiration and authority of the Bible, but considered together, they do portray a cumulative argument that I believe is hard to deny.

Let's look at the parts of this cumulative argument to see how they fit together.

1. The Bible says it is the inspired Word of God. This may seem like an obvious, self-serving statement, but I am amazed by how many people believe that the Bible never presents itself as God's Word. Somehow, they have missed all the passages in Scripture that affirm exactly that. Here are some examples:

- *2 Timothy 3:16-17* affirms "all Scripture is inspired by God and profitable for teaching, for reproof, for correction, for training in righteousness."

- *2 Peter 1:20-21* asserts that no prophecy in Scripture "was ever made by an act of human will, but men moved by the Holy Spirit spoke from God."

- In *1 Thessalonians 2:13* Paul claims that the Thessalonian Christians accepted what he presented to them "not *as* the word of men, but *for* what it really is, the word of God."

- *John the Apostle* in his Gospel records Jesus' teaching to his disciples that "if anyone loves Me, he will keep My word." Of course, the question is how can we know his word? Jesus goes on to say that after his death, the Father will send the Holy Spirit to them who "will teach you all things, and bring to your remembrance all that I said to you" (John 14:23-26). Many have wondered how the disciples could have possibly remembered what Jesus taught them and record it verbatim in the Gospels. This is how they could: the Holy Spirit brought to their remembrance everything Jesus had said, and taught them new things as well (see John 16:12-13). That is the essence of inspiration in the New Testament. It explains the origin of the Gospels ("remembrance") and of the Epistles ("all things") through the work of the Holy Spirit. That work of the Holy Spirit is what we call "inspiration."

There are many other passages in the New Testament on this subject, but let's look at some of the passages that deal with this issue in the Old Testament as well:

• In *Psalm 119* the psalmist talks repeatedly about God's Word. In verses 17-19, he speaks of God's Word, his law and his commandments. He asks God to "establish Your word to Your servant, / As that which produces reverence for You" (v. 38). The psalmist also promises that if God will teach him "the way of Your statutes" he will "observe it to the end" (v. 33). He also declares, "I trust in Your word" (v. 42); "I wait for Your ordinances" (v. 43); "I will keep Your law continually, / Forever and ever" (v. 44); and "I shall delight in Your commandments, / Which I love" (v. 47). Finally, the psalmist exults in his knowledge of God's Word,

> I have inherited Your testimonies forever,
> For they are the joy of my heart.
> I have inclined my heart to perform Your statutes
> Forever, even to the end. (vv. 111-112)

Whether the Word of God is identified as his commandments, his statutes, his testimonies, his law or his ordinances, the psalmist makes it clear that he believes in the inspiration and authority of the Word of God and gives his whole heart to obeying it because it brings him such joy. The entire psalm is a hymn of praise to God for his Word. I certainly share the psalmist's joy in God's Word and its effects in our lives!

- In *Isaiah 55* the prophet quotes God's teaching about his Word. God begins by saying that his thoughts and ways are not like ours; they are infinitely higher than ours (vv. 8-9). So how can we know God's ways and his thoughts? God explains that just

  > as the rain and the snow come down from heaven, . . .
  > So will My word be which goes forth from My mouth;
  > It will not return to Me empty,
  > Without accomplishing what I desire. (vv. 10-11)

  This is a beautiful picture of why we need God's revelation of his ways and his thoughts in order to live according to his will, and how he has accomplished that through the revelation of his Word. God has inspired and sent his Word to us so that we can know his thoughts and live accordingly.

  2. The consistency of the message of the Bible supports the probability of its inspiration by God. The Bible contains sixty-six books written during a period of more than 1,500 years by 40 different authors in 3 languages. Its diversities are legendary, yet its message is unified, coherent, interlocking, self-fulfilling and consistent throughout. If that doesn't prove the inspiration of God, it should certainly cause us to lean strongly in that direction!

  3. The amazing amount of fulfilled prophecy in the Bible speaks for its inspiration. There are more than 600 detailed prophecies in the Bible. The odds of their fulfillment are certainly slim. Dr. Peter W. Stoner, chair of the science department of Westmont College and a renowned professor of mathematics, has calculated that if you take only eight of the prophecies about Jesus, the probability of them being fulfilled in one person is an astounding one chance in 10^{17}! That means one chance in ten with seventeen zeroes after it![2] And that is just for eight prophecies; many more prophecies about Jesus were fulfilled in amazing detail. Again, that fact seems to incline toward the probability that the Bible is the inspired Word of God, and that it is unique among all the books of world literature.

  4. The confirmation of archaeological finds has bolstered faith in

the truthfulness of the Bible. There was a time when critics of the Bible loudly insisted that Solomon could not possibly have had the large number of horses the Bible says he had. But an archaeological find of thousands of horse stables near Jerusalem confirmed the Bible as true and silenced their attack. Many critics mocked the idea of Pharaoh's army drowning in the Red (or Reed) Sea until an amateur archaeologist, Ron Wyatt, found fossilized chariot wheels in the bottom of that sea. Critics also ridiculed the idea of the walls of Jericho collapsing as the people of Israel walked around it and blew their trumpets, but between 1952 and 1958 archaeologist Kathleen Kenyon did extensive investigations at the site of Jericho and found that the walls had collapsed just as the biblical text affirms. She also found that one of the walls on the northern side of Jericho had not collapsed. Many were puzzled by that finding until they remembered that God had promised Rahab that he would protect her and her home in the northern wall when the destruction came.

I could go on and on with examples like these in which archaeology has confirmed the truthfulness of the Bible. Suffice it to say that as of today, every single archaeological discovery has verified the biblical accounts.[3]

By the way, there is a myth going around that the Dead Sea Scrolls have proven that the New Testament is not true.[4] I have seen some of the scrolls personally, and the only thing that they have contributed to biblical scholarship is the assurance that, although they are the oldest manuscripts of the Old Testament we have, they match up virtually perfectly with the texts of the Hebrew Bible we have been using for more than a thousand years. Meanwhile, the Dead Sea Scrolls contain nothing from the New Testament in them! Far from causing doubts about the Bible, the Dead Sea Scrolls have increased our confidence in the reliability of the Old Testament text more than ever before.

5. When we compare the contents of the other two main religions' primary texts—Islam's Qur'an and the Hindu Mahabharata—the contrast is so stark that the Bible's inspiration by God becomes even more believable. The Qur'an is a fascinating book, full of contradictory commands, incitement to violence, hatred of nonbelievers and promises of carnal delights in Paradise. Above all that, Muhammad admitted in the text that some of the "revelations" that he believed he had received from God later proved to be "interjections of Satan" (sura 22:52). According to the translation of the Qur'an by M. H. Shakir the text of that passage reads, "Never did we send a messenger or a prophet before you but that when he recited (the Message) Satan cast words into his recitation (umniyyah). God abrogates what Satan casts. The God established his verses. God is knower, wise."[5] Sura 2:106 also states, "Whatever communications We abrogate or cause to be forgotten, We bring one better than it or like it. Do you not know that Allah has power over all things?" And sura 16:101 says, "And when We change (one) communication for (another) communication, and Allah knows best what he reveals, they say: You are only a forger. Nay, most of them do not know." This idea of abrogation or change of the text is the major Achilles' heel of Islam and the supposed dictational authority of its primary text. This admission by Muhammad that satanic interjections have crept into the Qur'an that had to be abrogated or eliminated later undermines the credibility of Muhammad's supposed revelations. Since the entire religion rests on the reliability of one man's assertion that God spoke his Word to him, it calls into question the entire foundation of that faith.

The Hindu Mahabharata is a mythological drama about how the world and humanity were produced. Not only are its descriptions difficult to believe, but so much of its content is sexual in nature that it seems to be almost obsessed with sex. I would illustrate that point, but I don't want this book to be rated "R" by the Christian community. Suffice it to say, Hinduism is a very sexual religion, and the Mahabharata condones and even encourages *devadasi*, the prostitution of young girls in Hindu temples. The "Project Combat" group estimates that there are still more than forty thousand girls serving as temple prostitutes in India today and that holy prostitution is still practiced in some remote parts of India.[6] Formerly, it was an integral part of Hindu religion but has now been outlawed by the Indian government.

Apparently enforcement of that law is almost impossible in some situations where Hindu religious tradition is still very strong. The fact that the Hindu sacred text encourages this barbaric practice illustrates the inferiority of its moral content.

Is it any wonder that those of us who have read all three books—the Bible, the Qur'an and the Mahabharata—come out concluding that the Bible is a qualitatively different kind of religious text? It does not contain "interjections from Satan," promotion of perverse sexual practices or arduous, elitist, self-atoning rituals. There really is no comparison.

6. *The accurate manuscript evidence supporting the Bible lends its support to the probability of its truthfulness and preservation over the centuries by God.* The pastor of the local Metaphysical Christianity church asked my students, "How can you believe in the Bible when you must know how much it has been corrupted over the centuries as it has been transmitted from generation to generation?" They later asked me if what he said was true; I was able to answer their questions the next day in class. Actually, the Old and New Testaments are the best-preserved works of ancient literature in existence today. There are more than 14,000 manuscripts of the Old Testament and 24,000 manuscripts of the New Testament. Meticulous study of those textual manuscripts has made it possible to affirm that the biblical text we now have is virtually an exact copy of the originals. The next best-attested ancient text—Homer's *Iliad*—has only 643 manuscripts in existence, and the earliest copy that exists was made nine hundred years after Homer wrote it. There is really no contest. The Bible is the best-preserved and best-attested book of ancient literature that exists today, without a doubt. It is not hard to believe in God's superintendence of the process of transmission of the Bible when you see those facts.

7. *The personal integrity and character of the authors of the Bible and the commitment they showed in giving their lives rather than deny the Bible's veracity also contribute to the belief that God has inspired their works.* The authors of the Gospels claim to be either eyewitnesses of the events they record or interviewers of actual eyewitnesses.

Either what they record is true or they (or their eyewitness sources) are liars or maniacs. When someone claims, as the apostle John did, that the message he shared was based on "what we have heard, what we have seen with our eyes, what we have looked at and touched with our hands" (1 John 1:1), you know that they want their readers to understand that they actually experienced what they are writing about. You can't get more "eyewitnessy" than that—heard, seen, looked at, touched!

Luke claims that his Gospel is based on interviews with eyewitnesses, since he was not one of the apostles:

> an account of the things accomplished among us, just as they were handed down to us *by those who from the beginning were eyewitnesses* and servants of the word, it seemed fitting for me as well, having investigated everything carefully from the beginning, to write *it* out for you in consecutive order, most excellent Theophilus; so that you may know the *exact truth* about the things you have been taught. (Luke 1:1-4, emphasis added)

The term *exact truth* that Luke uses here means "evidence based on eyewitness testimony worthy of the courtroom" (see Luke's use of this term in his second work, Acts). The eyewitness foundation of the Gospels is established. Matthew was an apostle and eyewitness, as was John. Mark was the apostle Peter's interpreter and disciple. Luke investigated everything he wrote about with the eyewitnesses of the events. They were all either eyewitnesses, disciples of eyewitnesses or interviewers of eyewitnesses. That is the source of the Gospels.

Further, the authors of the New Testament spoke out unequivocally against the use of myths, legends or fables in the Christian faith. For example, Peter writes, "We did not follow cleverly devised tales [myths] when we made known to you the power and coming of our Lord Jesus Christ, but we were eyewitnesses of His majesty" (2 Peter 1:16). And Paul tells Timothy not "to pay attention to myths" (1 Timothy 1:4), and "have nothing to do with worldly fables [myths]" (1 Timothy 4:7). Myths (stories invented to teach religious truths) are totally repudiated by the authors of the New Testament. They have no place in Christianity, which again makes the case for the truthfulness of the Gospels that much more reasonable.

Finally, the fact that most of the writers of the Bible were persecuted and many were killed for their insistence that the events recorded in the Bible were true lends a certain credibility of witness and commitment to their claims about the divinity of Jesus as attested by the apostolic witness in the New Testament. There are not many people who would give their lives to insist that what they know to be a lie is true. Certainly, the kind of charlatans who would falsify the texts for their own gain would not be likely candidates for standing up for things they know are false at the cost of their own lives.

8. The most subjective of all of these cumulative arguments is the effect the Bible has had on people's lives. Throughout history, when people have put into practice the teachings of the Bible, their lives have been changed for the better. They have become more loving, kind, generous, peaceful, faithful, pure, positive, disciplined, consistent, merciful, patient, benevolent, truthful and hopeful than they had ever been before. I would have to add my own word of testimony that God's Word, and God's use of it in me, has been the greatest agent for change in my life. I praise God for it with all my heart!

Let me close this chapter by sharing the testimony of Bob Wilkerson, pastor and evangelist, whose life was touched by the power of the Word of God in such a dramatic way when he was in jail:

> The jail cell was nasty and green with crud all over the walls. Once again, I was in Jail awaiting my arraignment. I was guilty of DUI so going to court didn't really mean anything to me. I would be fined, ordered to go to class, be put on probation and lose my license for three years. If I got one more, I would have to serve a year in prison.
>
> Years ago, I had this spiritual experience with Jesus Christ, read the bible, went to church, and even worked in the church. However, since that time I had been in jail many times, com-

mitted to mental institutions and detoxed for alcohol and drug abuse so many times I can't even remember.

This visit to jail turned out to be different. I was considered hopeless and all the people I knew had given up on me. Even the doctors had given up; I was doomed to die a horrible death from addiction. Yet, those who gave up on me forgot about a friend I met years ago.

There was a black guard in the jail system. Every day he came by, stood out side my cell, and sang a song about Jesus. Weird, it was weird. I remember crying; hoping God would help me. The guard told me if I ask God to help, he would. The next thing the guard did was put a green bible through the hole in the cell door. I still have the bible and word Sheriff's Annex written on the side.

Anyway, I started reading the book. I mean I didn't just read it I absorbed the words. I began to claim the promises in the bible and they began to work for me. After being released I still kept reading the bible. I stayed sober and I began to change. I surrendered to Jesus again and gave my life to him. Jesus and the word of God worked when nothing else did. I really don't care what you think, it worked or I would be dead.

Today, years later, I still read the word and I still practice the principles in the bible. Oh, I am not perfect and no one said I had to be perfect. However, I do trust in Jesus and I do believe the word of God has the power to change a life when applied and practiced.[7]

That testimony sums up the power of the Word of God when it is read, believed and practiced!

These eight arguments are not conclusive one by one, but when they are combined (like the components of a house) the effect of their cumulative power is unmistakable. When you put together the power of the Bible's self-identification as God's inspired Word, the consistency of its message, its many fulfilled prophecies, unanimous archaeological confirmations, favorable comparison with other religious texts, massive manuscript evidence, the integrity of its authors, and its effect on countless lives throughout history, Christians have ample reason to believe that this book is the inspired Word of God.

PRAYING THE PRINCIPLE

Lord, teach me to believe in your Word as Your love letter to me, and live out its principles in every part of my daily life to your glory and for my good.

> All Scripture is inspired by God and profitable for teaching, for reproof, for correction, for training in righteousness; so that the man of God may be adequate, equipped for every good work. (2 Timothy 3:16-17)

DISCUSSING THE PRINCIPLE

1. Why would anyone believe the Bible is the inspired Word of God? Why is this *the* foundational question for Christian faith?

2. What does the Bible say about its own inspiration?

3. How would you summarize the eight arguments for the inspiration of the Bible?

4. Is there someone with whom you should share them? If so, name the person(s).

5. How does the inspiration of God's Word affect your daily life?

2

Isn't the Bible
Full of Contradictions?

The issue of contradictions in the Bible came alive to me in a seminary class on New Testament Greek. The professor, who was the most liberal professor in a fairly conservative seminary, was showing us different versions of the same event in the three Synoptic Gospels (Matthew, Mark, Luke) in Greek—the calming of the storm when Jesus and his disciples were crossing the Sea of Galilee. He painstakingly had us look at each passage in the original Greek and compare them. He especially wanted us to notice the expressions of terror shouted by the disciples and how different they were in each passage. In Matthew 8:25 they said, "Save us, Lord; we are perishing." But in Mark 4:38 they said, "Teacher, do You not care that we are perishing?" Finally, in Luke 8:24 they said, "Master, Master, we are perishing!" After emphasizing the startling differences between the three accounts, and knowing that I had often argued with him in class in favor of the truthfulness of the New Testament, he turned to me and said, "Well, Mr. Hundley, what does that do to your view of truth in the New Testament?" I answered, smiling, "Not one thing, professor." He roared back, "Why not?" "Well, because if my Greek is right, in every case the verb is plural, and I find it hard to believe that twelve men in a boat that was sinking would all stand up together and cry out in unison using the exact same words! In fact, I suspect that they probably cried out twelve different things, not just three." His face turned red as the other students howled with laughter. He quickly switched to another topic.

What had happened? An apparent contradiction in the text, one of that professor's favorites, had been shown to be completely false. I have spent the last forty years of my life doing that same thing with professors and with authors of books who attempt to discredit God's Word by claiming that it is full of contradictions and therefore can't possibly be true. During my three years at the University of Cambridge, I was constantly assailed by people who were convinced that the Bible is full of contradictions. I never found even one of the cases that they presented that could not convincingly be explained as noncontradictory. I want to share with you four of the principles I have found to be particularly helpful in understanding these apparent "contradictions."

FOUR PRINCIPLES THAT EXPLAIN APPARENT CONTRADICTIONS

1. The principle of translation. Jesus did not speak Greek; he spoke Aramaic. So everything in the Gospels is a translation from Aramaic into Greek. This principle accounts for some of the minor discrepancies between verses. At one time I was a Spanish translator. In a session to prepare us for the translator's accreditation exam, the leader put an English sentence on the board and asked each of us to translate it into Spanish. We then were asked to write our translations on the board underneath the English sentence. Each of our translations was unique. We all had the gist of the sentence, but none of us used the exact same words in Spanish to translate it. The leader spent the rest of the hour picking through each translation, showing how it could be improved. She did tell us that we had all communicated the meaning of the original sentence fairly well, but she insisted that only one of our translations was totally correct. Suffice it to say, translation from Aramaic to Greek and from Greek to English produces many variations in the wording of texts, but *they do not constitute true contradictions.*

2. The principle of similar teachings. Often, Jesus repeated the same teaching on a subject, giving basically the same content in different settings. Some critics want to say that these are contradictions because he either said it in one setting or another, but not both. That is not necessarily true. One of the most famous examples of this is Jesus' teaching on divorce. In Matthew 5:31-32 Jesus presents his view on divorce as part of the "Sermon on the Mount." But in Mark 10:10-12 Jesus gives the same teaching when some of the Pharisees ask him about it—no "mount." Again, this is a case of similar teachings in different settings, not a contradiction.

I have given the same basic sermon on how to know the will of God in the United States, in Colombia, in Nicaragua, in Russia and in England, but it has been essentially the same message every time. Could it be that two thousand years from now critics will look at those different settings with the same basic content and conclude that there are contradictions between them and therefore some of them are fabrications? I don't think they should, but that is what has happened with many passages in the Bible. *I don't see those as contradictions either.*

3. The principle of simultaneous actions. One critic pointed out to me that there was a contradiction in the narrations of Jesus' baptism. In Matthew 3:17 God shows his approval of Jesus as he is baptized by saying, "This is My beloved Son, in whom I am well-pleased." But in Mark 1:11 God says, "You are My beloved Son, in You I am well-pleased." Luke goes along with Mark's version. "See," the critic insisted, "they can't both be true. That is an obvious contradiction in the text." I told him that was not necessarily so. Had he ever considered that in such an important event in the life of Jesus, God might have wanted to give an outward testimony to those present, but also give an inward word of personal commendation to his Son? Both communications could have occurred at the same moment, one outward and one inward. Matthew emphasizes God's witness of approval to the crowd, while Mark and Luke emphasize God's approval given directly to his Son, Jesus. There are many cases like this in which two things happen at the same time, one noted by one Gospel writer and one noted by another, *but they are not contradictions.*

4. The principle of harmonizing details. No one Gospel writer claims to have included all the details of any event in Jesus' life. Yet some critics claim that there are contradictions if one Gospel has fewer or more details about an event than another one. This seems patently illogical to me. If two or three people today saw the same traffic accident, would you expect that all of them would give exactly the same details in the police officer's report? Of course not. They would each have noted certain details depending on their vantage point, personal experience and interests. One might say the driver had on a blue shirt, another that his shirt was flannel, and the third that his shirt was torn. But they would all be right. They are giving complementary details about what they saw. That is often the case in parallel passages in the Gospels. *Again, those should not be considered to be contradictions by any reasonable person.*

Many of the supposed contradictions claimed by critics of the Bible can be easily explained away using these four principles. I reserve judgment about those that can't until I get further knowledge. But there are very few in that category.[1]

PRAYING THE PRINCIPLE

Lord, I praise you for the trustworthiness of your Word. You have given us real events that took place in real time and space and you have preserved them in an inerrant record that inspires confidence, trust and faith. I praise you for your desire to communicate to us in such a wonderful way. I know in my heart, in my mind and in my experience of life that your Word is truth!

Establish Your word to Your servant,
As that which produces reverence for You. . . .

I will have an answer for him who reproaches me,
For I trust in Your word. (Psalm 119:38, 42)

Sanctify them in the truth; Your word is truth. (John 17:17)

DISCUSSING THE PRINCIPLE

1. Briefly summarize the four principles that explain apparent contradictions in the text of the New Testament, offering biblical or common experience examples of each one.

2. What books by Norman Geisler and Gleason L. Archer give further explanations about the noncontradictory nature of the Scriptures (see endnotes)?

3. How would you answer someone who said the New Testament is full of contradictions?

3

Why Were the Books of the Bible Accepted as Scripture, but Other Books Were Not?

It is in vogue today to question the selection of the books of the Bible. Movies like *Stigmata* and books like *The Da Vinci Code* have made many people question whether the books in the Bible should actually be accepted as authoritative or whether other books should have been included in the Bible. In the scholarly world the writings of two women have had a profound effect on this issue. Princeton's Elaine Pagels has questioned the traditional books of the New Testament in her books *The Gnostic Gospels* (1979) and *Beyond Belief: The Secret Gospel of Thomas* (2004). Harvard's Karen L. King has taken a similar tack in her book *What Is Gnosticism?* (2003). The two women collaborated in 2007 to write *Reading Judas: The Gospel of Judas and the Shaping of Christianity*. Because of the Jesus Seminar movement, their doubts about the authority and legitimacy of biblical books have received wide distribution.[1]

THE JESUS SEMINAR

I attended a Jesus Seminar meeting a few years ago and heard Karen King explain her unorthodox theories. As she championed the Gospel of Mary as equal to the four Gospels, she made it quite clear that she was speaking as a feminist theologian. During the open Q&A session, I asked her how she could be sure she wasn't trying to defend the validity of the Gospel of Mary merely because it reinforced her own feminist theological position. I ended my question by asking if she and the other theologians in the Jesus Seminar movement had established safeguards to make sure that they weren't (as José Míguez Bonino has warned) merely "hearing the echo of their own ideology in Scripture, which muzzles the Word of God."[2] She chose not to answer my question, but deferred to a colleague in the seminar, who avoided it as well.

Whether popularized in movies and fiction or studiously defended in scholarly academic volumes, the idea that the books of the Bible are not there for valid reasons and that other books which should be there have been arbitrarily excluded is gaining ground every day. Christians must know what they believe about this and be ready to defend their faith in God's Word.

EPHESIANS 2 AND THE FOUNDATION OF NEW TESTAMENT FAITH

There is a crucial passage in Paul's epistle to the Ephesians which will help us get a handle on this issue. Paul says that the Ephesians responded to the gospel and were made "fellow citizens with the saints" and part of "God's household" (Ephesians 2:19). In the next verse Paul declares that the "household of God" has "been built on the foundation of the *apostles and prophets*, Christ Jesus himself being the corner *stone*" (emphasis added). Here, Paul is echoing the New Testament fundamental belief that the Christian faith is based on the authority and writings of two groups: the apostles and the prophets.

Prophets refers mainly to the prophets of the Old Testament (although there are a few prophets in the New Testament). The New Testament records several descriptions of prophets from the Old Testament, including Enoch, Jonah, Daniel, Jeremiah, Isaiah, Elisha, Joel and Samuel. The crowds in the New Testament also refer to Jesus as a prophet (Matthew 21:11; Mark 6:15; Luke 7:16; John 7:40). The Old Testament books were included in the canon (the authoritative list of biblical books) on the basis of having been written by a prophet. The Old Testament identifies many prophets, including Moses, Aaron, Balaam, Samuel, Gad, Nathan, David, Ahijah, Jehu, Elijah, Elisha, Micaiah, Jonah, Shemaiah, Iddo, Oded, Eliezer, Zechariah, Jeremiah, Uriah, Ezekiel, Daniel, Hosea, Amos, Habakkuk, Haggai, Miriam and Deborah. These men and women are those through whom God spoke. That's what it means to be a prophet. God speaks to the prophet and the prophet speaks to the people in God's name.

Matthew describes the process: "what was spoken by the Lord through the prophet" (Matthew 1:22; 2:15). What a fascinating idea: God speaks to us through a person chosen by him for that purpose! Often, in the Old Testament the prophet begins a message with "thus says the LORD" to emphasize the fact that the message is not the prophet's but God's (see, for example, 2 Chronicles 12:5; Ezekiel 36:3). I am particularly impressed with the humility of the prophet Amos who, when he is accused of treason for the message he has been preaching, responds, "the LORD took me from following the flock and the LORD said to me, 'Go prophesy to My people Israel.' Now hear the word of the LORD" (Amos 7:15-16). That is the essence of what it means to be a prophet: a man or woman chosen by God to speak God's word to the people.

There were also false prophets who pretended to be speaking for God, but actually were lying. They were rejected; in fact, some were executed (see, for example, Deuteronomy 18:20; Jeremiah 29:31-32; Zechariah 13:2-3). Their false prophecies are included in the Old Testament as examples of the difference between true prophecy and false prophecy.

THE AUTHORITY OF THE OLD TESTAMENT

The authority of the Old Testament is fully based on the foundation of the authority of the prophets who spoke for God. The Old Testament is the recording of (1) the messages they brought (Isaiah, Jeremiah, Ezekiel, Amos, etc.), (2) the narrative that tells the history of the people of Israel and how God dealt with them (Samuel, Kings, Chronicles, etc.), and (3) dramatic and poetic expressions of Hebrew peoples' faith and their struggles as they tried to follow God (Job, Psalms, Proverbs, Ecclesiastes, etc.).

Roland K. Harrison, in his classic work *Introduction to the Old Testament*, explains that "in summary, only those works which could properly claim prophetic authorship had a legitimate right to canonicity [in the Hebrew Bible]."[3] Harrison also clarifies that in the process of producing the Hebrew canon, the people of Israel considered Moses to be the author of Job. Samuel was accepted to be the author of Judges and Ruth. Jeremiah was credited with the authorship of Kings and Lamentations, and Ezra the scribe was believed to be the author of 1–2 Chronicles. Esther was admitted because Mordecai was accepted as a prophet at the time of Haggai, Zechariah and Malachi, "and he was held to have prophesied at the time of Darius I."[4] In summary, every book in the Hebrew Bible that was accepted into the canon of the Old Testament was selected because its author was considered to be a prophet.

Jewish people today still refer to the three parts of the Hebrew Bible as Torah, the Prophets and the Writings. The Hebrew Bible is called the Tanakh, which is an acrostic that refers to the three letters: T (Torah), N (Nevi'im—prophets) and K (Ketuvim—writings). Together, they form the God-spoken Hebrew Bible which God revealed through his prophets to his people.

THE AUTHORITY OF THE NEW TESTAMENT

The New Testament is based on the writings of the apostles. New Testament books were accepted on the basis of *apostolicity*: the idea that a book is written either by an apostle of Christ (one of the twelve plus Paul) or by the disciple of an apostle. Which books were written by apostles? They are Matthew, John (including his Gospel, epistles and Revelation), Peter's epistles, Jude and James. Paul was considered to be an apostle, even though he was not one of the original twelve disciples of Jesus, because the Lord called him to be an apostle after his resurrection (see Galatians 1:1; 2:8). Luke was the disciple of Paul, so Luke and Acts are covered. Luke also makes it clear that he investigated everything in his Gospel with the eyewitnesses of the events. Mark was the disciple of Peter; in fact, he was his interpreter and based his Gospel on Peter's preaching.[5] That only leaves the epistle to the Hebrews, which was accepted because it was believed to have been written either by Paul or one of his disciples. (It may well have been written by Paul's disciple Barnabas, but we can't prove that for sure.)

In the New Testament there is a clear presentation of how God's Word came through the apostles and their disciples. Jesus promised in John 14 and 16 that after his death, God would send the disciples the Holy Spirit, "the Spirit of truth," who would help them (John 14:16-17). He tells them that if they love him, they will "keep [his] word," and that as a result, he and the Father will come to that person and "make Our abode with him" (John 14:23). But this amazing promise is based on their ability to remember his word and obey it. How could they possibly do that? Jesus explains to them that "the Helper, the Holy Spirit, whom the Father will send in My name, He will teach you all things, and bring to your remembrance all that I said to you" (John 14:26). They would be enabled supernaturally by the Holy Spirit to remember what Jesus said to them! That's where the Gospels come from. The Gospels are the Holy Spirit-supplied recollections of the words and acts of Jesus Christ.

Then, in John 16, Jesus goes on to tell them, "I have many more things to say to you, but you cannot bear *them* now. But when He, the Spirit of truth, comes, He will guide you into all the truth; . . . and He will disclose to you what is to come" (John 16:12-13). Here we see Jesus' provision, through the Holy Spirit, of the three basic parts of the New Testament: the Gospels ("bring to your remembrance all that I said to you"), the Epistles ("He will guide you into all truth"), and the prophetic parts of the New Testament and the book of the Revelation ("disclose to you what is to come"). Jesus made sure that his apostles would have all they needed to write the New Testament under the inspiration of the Holy Spirit. That, of course, is exactly what they did.

This apostolic authority, evidenced in the "credentials of an apostle" ("the signs of a true apostle . . . signs and wonders and miracles" [2 Corinthians 12:11-12]), became the authoritative foundation of the early Christian church. The book of Acts records that the earliest Christians recognized the authority of the apostles and "were continually devoting themselves to the apostles' teaching" (Acts 2:42). Peter saw his epistles as an extension of his apostolic ministry that would continue on after his death: "knowing that the laying aside of my *earthly* dwelling is imminent, as also our Lord Jesus Christ has made clear to me. And I will also be diligent that at any time after my departure you will be able to call these things to mind" (2 Peter 1:14-15). Paul describes his own ministry to the Thessalonians as giving them the very Word of God when he says, "we also constantly thank God that when you received the word of God which you heard from us, you accepted *it* not *as* the word of men, but *for* what it really is, the word of God" (1 Thessalonians 2:13). The apostles fulfilled the ministry that Jesus prophesied they would have in John 14 and 16.

So, in answer to the first part of our question, the books in the Old Testament were accepted because they were written by prophets who spoke for God, and the books of the New Testament were accepted because they were either written by one of the twelve apostles (plus Paul, whose apostolic call came from the resurrected Jesus [Galatians 1:11-12, 15-17; Romans 1:1] and was confirmed by his miraculous ministry [2 Corinthians 11:5–12:11]) or by a disciple of an apostle under that apostle's supervision. Now, how about the second part of the question: why weren't other books accepted?

WHY OTHER BOOKS WERE NOT ACCEPTED IN THE BIBLE

Regarding the Old Testament, there are seven books that were not accepted as canonical and authoritative because of doubts concerning their authors. Those books are commonly referred to as the Apocrypha (or deuterocanonical books). They include Tobit, Judith, Wisdom, Sirach, Baruch and 1–2 Maccabees, plus some additions to Esther, Jeremiah and Daniel (such as Song of the Three Children,

Story of Susanna, and Bel and the Dragon). Although they are not considered to be equal to the other books of the Old Testament, they do offer some interesting insights into the history of the period between the writing of the Old and New Testaments. However, as a response to the Reformation, the Roman Catholic Church held a council in Trent from 1545 to 1563, and out of their deliberations they accepted the Apocrypha as equal in authority to the rest of the Old Testament. They believed that some of those books gave support to the Catholic doctrine of purgatory, which Reformer Martin Luther opposed. Because of that decision, Catholics accept those seven books as an integral part of the Old Testament, but Protestants do not. Following their own long tradition, Jews have never accepted the Apocrypha as part of the Hebrew Bible.

The books that were rejected from the New Testament were not allowed to be part of the Christian official canon because they lacked apostolicity. That is, they were not written either by an apostle or the disciple of an apostle. They were written in the second century, after the death of the last apostle. Many of them, like the *Gospel of Thomas*, directly contradicted the plain teaching of the New Testament. A partial list of those rejected books would include the *Gospel of Truth, Gospel of Mary, Gospel of Thomas, Gospel of Philip* and *Gospel of Judas*. Many of those apocryphal books were attributed to apostles, but the church knew they were not written by an apostle, and so they were rejected.[6] Great care was taken to include only those books that met the requirement of apostolicity.

Two key passages in the New Testament give very clear pictures of how God used these men to deliver his Word. Peter summarized the process of inspiration by saying that "no prophecy was ever made by an act of human will, but men moved by the Holy Spirit spoke from God" (2 Peter 1:21). Paul also summed up this concept writing: "All Scripture is inspired [in Greek, *theopneustos*, which means God-breathed] by God and profitable for teaching, for reproof, for correction, for training in righteousness; so that the man of God may be adequate, equipped for every good work" (2 Timothy 3:16-17). Those two passages provide the basic concept behind the Old and New Testament books: they were given through those who spoke for God under his direct inspiration—*prophets* and *apostles*. Their ministries and the works they wrote under the inspiration of the Holy Spirit form the firm foundation for the Christian faith. That is the origin of the Bible.

PRAYING THE PRINCIPLE

I praise You, Lord, for the way you inspired your prophets and apostles to produce your wonderful Word. I happily submit my life to its principles and joyously seek to share its riches with others who, like me, are looking for a word from you about how to live our lives.

> But you, beloved, ought to remember the words that were spoken beforehand by the apostles of our Lord Jesus Christ, that they were saying to you, "In the last time there will be mockers, following after their own ungodly lusts." These are the ones who cause divisions, worldly-minded, devoid of the Spirit. (Jude 17-19)

DISCUSSING THE PRINCIPLE

1. What was the role of the prophets in the production of the Old Testament?

2. What is *apostolicity* and how did it determine what books would be accepted into the New Testament canon?

3. What did Jesus promise the apostles in John 14 and 16, and what does the fulfillment of that promise have to do with the writing of the New Testament?

4. Why were the apocryphal books and other "Gospels" not included in the Old Testament?

5. What do 2 Peter 1:21 and 2 Timothy 3:16-17 teach about the inspiration of the authors of the Bible?

4

Can We Believe in
the Biblical Account of the
Resurrection of Jesus?

In the 1700s two Oxford students met to discuss their mutual loathing for the Christian faith, which they described as a "tale gone mad." They made a pact to destroy Christianity once and for all by proving that the two pillars it is based on are false: the resurrection of Jesus and the conversion of Saul of Tarsus. Lord George Lyttelton chose to refute the conversion of Paul, and Gilbert West elected to prove the falseness of the biblical account of Jesus' resurrection. They met at Oxford after dedicating their long vacation to arduous research and writing. When they came together again in the fall semester, they had both become Christians! In 1747 West published his book *Observations on the History and Evidences of the Resurrection of Jesus Christ*. In it he argues meticulously for the historical truthfulness of the biblical account of the resurrection of Jesus. Lord Lyttelton wrote a book titled *Observations on the Conversion and Apostleship of Saint Paul*, proving the validity of Paul's conversion and sharing his new-found faith. Those two skeptics became convinced believers.

PROFESSOR GREENLEAF AND THE RESURRECTION

Dr. Simon Greenleaf was professor of law at Harvard University. He was the author of the three-volume classic work *A Treatise on the Law of Evidence*, which although written in 1842 is considered to be one of the best treatments of the topic of legal evidence ever written, even today. He was skeptical about the trustworthiness of Christianity and readily shared his skepticism with his students. Professor Greenleaf had some Christian students in his class who were tired of his attacks on the Christian faith. One day they met with him and asked him if he would consider applying his book's rules of evidence to the New Testament account of the historical resurrection of Jesus Christ. He agreed to do so, and after a painstaking study of the evidence he wrote a book titled *An Examination of the Testimony of the Four Evangelists by the Rules of Evidence Administered in the Courts of Justice*, in which he stated, "If the evidence for the resurrection was set before any unbiased courtroom in the world it would be judged to be an historical fact—Jesus rose from the dead!" Greenleaf became a believer too.

LEE STROBEL: FROM SKEPTIC TO BELIEVER

In our day hard-nosed journalist Lee Strobel followed a similar path to faith. As a reporter for the *Chicago Tribune* Strobel had covered many horrific events. He was a spiritual skeptic who rejected the Christian faith, but his wife's conversion challenged him to study Christianity to either disprove it or confirm it for himself. After his study and subsequent conversion to Christianity, Strobel wrote *The Case for Christ: A Journalist's Personal Investigation of the Evidence for Jesus*, which is an exceptional book recounting his spiritual journey and supporting the evidence for the truthfulness of Christian claims.

I could give many more cases of individuals who have set out to disprove the resurrection of Christ only to end up as believers, but there are also many people who have attacked the resurrection and refused to believe in it, offering various theories about what really happened.

THEORIES OF THOSE WHO REJECT THE RESURRECTION

1. The disciples stole the body. The Jewish refutation of the Christian faith, known as the Toledot Yeshu, probably began to circulate orally in the second century. It was written down by the fourth century. In it the writers support the theory that Jesus' body was stolen by his disciples, who then falsely proclaimed his resurrection. Actually, the "stolen body explanation" is mentioned in the New Testament.

Matthew 28 describes what happened when Jesus rose from the dead. An earthquake took place as an angel removed the stone from the tomb. The temple guard, who were Roman soldiers, have been sent by the Jewish leaders to make sure that the disciples could not steal the body of Jesus and proclaim a false resurrection (see Matthew 27:62-66). Seeing the angel the temple guards trembled with fear and then fainted. When the guards came to, they ran into the city to report to the chief priests what had happened. The Jewish chief priests and elders gave the soldiers "a large sum of money" and told them to say, "His disciples came by night and stole Him away while we were asleep" (see Matthew 28:2-4, 11-15). The text says that the soldiers took the money and did as they were told, so that "this story was widely spread among the Jews, *and is* to this day."

There are clear problems with the theory that the disciples stole Jesus' body.

- *Where did the disciples' courage come from?* They all ran away in fear when Jesus was arrested. How could they marshal the courage to face Roman soldiers, steal the body and then risk their lives to proclaim the resurrection even though they knew it never happened?

- *How could eleven men move a one-ton stone while Roman soldiers slept and not awaken them?* Surely they would have made some sound accomplishing that Herculean task!

- *If the Roman soldiers were asleep, how could they possibly know that Jesus' disciples stole the body?* Anyone could have done it, so how could they identify the perpetrators when they were supposedly sleeping?

- *The penalty for sleeping on duty for a Roman soldier was being burned alive.* Why would the soldiers fall asleep, and worse, why would they admit to it?

- *Why didn't Jesus' many Roman and Jewish enemies search for and find his body, and then produce it to destroy Christianity?* They knew who Jesus' disciples were. Why didn't they seek them out and find his body? They could have destroyed Christianity with one fatal blow, but they didn't because they couldn't. His body was resurrected!

2. The swoon theory. Made popular at the end of the eighteenth century by German theologian Karl Friedrich Bahrdt, the swoon theory suggests that Jesus did not actually die on the cross. He merely appeared to be dead because he swooned or fainted. In the tomb he was revived when the spices were applied to his body, and he escaped and probably lived out his days in an Essene community.

Problems that arise from the swoon theory:

- *The Roman soldiers were experienced executioners.* How could they mistakenly think Jesus was dead when he wasn't? Further, if Jesus had only swooned, why didn't he react when the spear was thrust into his side?

- *How did Jesus escape from the tomb with the sealed stone in front of it and a contingent of Roman soldiers guarding it?* If he had swooned from his wounds, he would have been in a weakened condition. How could he possibly have removed the stone, avoided the soldiers and escaped?

- *If Jesus escaped to an Essene community in the desert, how do they account for the eyewitness testimony of more than five hundred people that saw him alive in Jerusalem after his death* (see 1 Corinthians 15:6)?

3. The Passover plot. In his book *The Passover Plot*, author Hugh Schonfield proposes the theory that while on the cross Jesus, with the help of Joseph of Arimathea, received a drug mixed in with the vinegar, which made him appear to be dead. But then he later recovered and escaped. Fully recovered from the drug-induced state, Jesus presented himself to people and claimed to be the Messiah. Schonfield says that Jesus' disciples claimed that he had risen from the dead, even though they knew it wasn't true.

Problems with the view that Jesus revived from a drugged state and escaped:

- *If Jesus recovered from the drug-induced state in the tomb, how did he get out of it?*
- *How did he get past the Roman soldiers?*
- *If Jesus was in Jerusalem claiming to be the Messiah, why didn't the Jewish or Roman authorities arrest him and put an end to his fraud?*
- *If what Schonfield says is true, Jesus was certainly the most diabolical, despicable character in all of history.* How could that kind of person have inspired the kind of devotion that his disciples showed by risking their lives to proclaim his resurrection?

4. The vision theory. Some skeptics have tried to explain away the resurrection by suggesting that Jesus' disciples experienced a hallucination or vision of his risen form, which they mistakenly thought was real. This "mass hysteria" is explained on the basis of those individuals' disappointment at his death and fervent desire to see him again.

Problems inherent in the vision theory:

- *What explanation can be given for a "mass hysteria" in which more than five hundred people, in different places and at different dates, had the same vision?* It is illogical to posit a shared vision for so many people in so many different settings.

- *Would a mere vision of the resurrected Jesus tell Thomas to put his finger in Jesus' hands and his hand in Jesus' side? And would a vision eat breakfast with the disciples?* John 20:24-29 affirms that Jesus proved himself to Thomas in a very physical way, not as a vision or a spirit. In Luke 24:36-43, when Jesus appears before his disciples, they actually think he is a spirit of some kind. Jesus answers their fear by saying, "See My hands and My feet, that it is I Myself; touch me and see, for a spirit does not have flesh and bones as you see that I have." He showed them his hands and feet, but they still "could not believe it because of their joy and amazement." So, Jesus asked them if they had anything to eat, and they gave him some broiled fish and he ate it in front of them. No vision or spirit could do that!

- *If the resurrection were just a vision, why did the apostles proclaim it as an historical event?* According to the apostolic witness, the people that experienced Jesus after his resurrection had very concrete, physical encounters with him. They saw him, heard him, touched him, ate with him, and examined his hands and feet for the scars of the crucifixion. As the apostles spread the good news, they constantly referred to the resurrection of Jesus as a real event. That claim appears eleven times in the book of Acts as part of their preaching. Being an eyewitness of Jesus' resurrection was a requirement for the candidate chosen to take Judas' place as the twelfth apostle (Acts 1:21-22). Paul insisted that if the resurrection did not actually take place, Christianity was "worthless" (1 Corinthians 15:17). These pronouncements make it very difficult, if not impossible, to believe that the faith they proclaimed, and for which they gave their lives, was only based on some visions resulting from wishful thinking and mass hysteria.

SUMMARY: JESUS ROSE FROM THE DEAD!

Those simple questions addressed to the main opponents of the resurrection make it abundantly clear that their proposals are not plausible explanations of what happened. And if Jesus' body was not stolen by his disciples, nor did he faint and then revive and escape, nor did he take a drug and fake his death, nor was the resurrection simply a vision shared by hundreds of people, then what did happen? The only genuine conclusion is that *Jesus rose from the dead!*

So, let's summarize some of the reasons why Christians believe that the resurrection of Jesus Christ actually took place:

1. The apostles testified that it happened. Not only were they not the kind of people to lie about such a thing, but most of them gave their lives for proclaiming Jesus' resurrection.

2. Something very earth-shattering must have taken place in Jeru-

salem to cause Jewish believers and even Jewish priests to leave their faith (and ministry!) to join what many considered to be a heretical religious group (Acts 6:7). Nothing less than the resurrection of Jesus could have caused that to happen.

3. The Jewish leaders, with the help of the Roman guards, made it absolutely impossible for there to be a fake resurrection. They sealed the tomb so that anyone disturbing the stone would break the seal and reveal their tampering. They set a contingent of Roman guards in front of the tomb to make sure that no one could possibly steal the body and fake a resurrection. The best story the Jewish leaders could come up with, which they paid the guards to publicize, is ludicrous in the extreme, for reasons we have already seen. So, thanks to the Jewish leaders' desire to thwart a fake resurrection, we can be assured that the resurrection actually took place, just as the apostles said it did.

4. The stone placed at the entrance to the tomb probably weighed between one and two tons, and was wedged into place on an incline. A man recovering from wounds and being drugged, as some claim Jesus was, would have been completely incapable of moving such an object. And the disciples could not have moved it without awakening the guards.

5. Jesus' enemies knew from the guards that the resurrection had taken place, so they concocted a false explanation so that no one would believe it. However, they never exhibited Jesus' body or exposed him as being alive in some other place to give a death blow to Christianity. If they could have done that, they would have, but they couldn't because he rose from the dead.

6. The eyewitness testimony of more than five hundred people who saw Jesus after his resurrection gives ample proof that it really took place.

7. Jesus foretold his death and resurrection to his disciples on many occasions.

8. Far from plotting to "sell" the resurrection, the disciples had to be convinced to believe that it had actually happened. When they first saw Jesus, they were scared to death and thought he was a ghost. If someone were to make up a story like this, would they create it in such a way that they looked weak, pathetic and unbelieving?

9. In the book of Acts, Jewish leaders often attacked the apostles for preaching the gospel, but they never tried to refute the resurrection. Apparently, general knowledge of the empty tomb caused them to give up that approach. Their silence speaks as loudly as the preaching of the apostles.

10. Millions of people through the centuries and around the world have met the living Christ and their lives have been dramatically transformed by his resurrection power! I am one of those people.

THE RESURRECTION AND THE UNIQUENESS OF THE CHRISTIAN FAITH

The resurrection of Jesus Christ makes Christianity unique among all the world religions. As G. B. Hardy has written in his book *Countdown*:

> Here is the complete record:
>
> Confucius' tomb—occupied
> Buddha's tomb—occupied
> Mohammed's tomb—occupied
> Jesus' tomb—EMPTY![1]

The founder of no other religion came back from the dead to help his followers live their lives in his power. I am convinced that the proofs of the truthfulness of Jesus' resurrection should be sufficient for anyone who has an open mind. And let's be clear: If Jesus did rise from the dead and is alive today, we all need to come to terms with him and his claim on our lives. The living Christ is inviting us to get to know him in all of his glory and power. We dare not reject his gracious offer.

THE PROMISE OF RESURRECTION POWER

Finally, I believe that one of the greatest promises in all of the New Testament is found in Ephesians 1:18-20. It states that the same power of God that raised Jesus from the dead is now at work in and through Christians! How much power does it take to restore life to a corpse? A great deal! Well, that same power is now operating inside of every Christian believer. If we can plug in to that *resurrection power*, God can do great things in and through our lives! The resurrection of Jesus means that death does not have the final victory, Satan is defeated, Jesus is confirmed to be God's Son, the promises of Jesus' resurrection are true, and the power of his resurrection is at work in each of our lives as we serve him and rejoice in his resurrected life!

Christianity without the resurrection would be a mere collection of beautiful thoughts given by a special man, but with the resurrection the gospel is "the power of God for salvation" (Romans 1:16), and our firm confidence is that the God who raised Jesus from the dead will also give life to our mortal bodies one day, and we will see him again with the nail prints in his hands and feet, and gratefully worship him forever.[2]

PRAYING THE PRINCIPLE

Lord, thank you for the living hope that since you brought Jesus back from the dead, you will do the same for us the day we die. Your resurrection power is so awesome. There is truly nothing that can stop you, not even death! I praise you that Jesus' resurrection is a reality and your Word makes it clear that it could not be otherwise.

Blessed be the God and Father of our Lord Jesus Christ, who according to His great mercy has caused us to be born again to a living hope through the resurrection of Jesus Christ from the dead. (1 Peter 1:3)

DISCUSSING THE PRINCIPLE

1. What happened to journalist Lee Strobel through his critical study of Christianity?

2. What are the four most common theories used to refute the resurrection, and what are some important questions for the proponents of each theory to answer?

3. Briefly summarize the ten reasons why Christians believe that the resurrection of Jesus Christ actually took place.

4. How does the resurrection make Christianity unique among all world religions?

5. What is the awesome promise in Ephesians 1:18-20, and how does it apply to your life?

6. How has belief in the resurrection of Jesus changed your life?

PART TWO

Questions About Doctrine

Once we have established the trustworthiness and divine inspiration of the Bible, the next step in the Christian life is to consider the teaching that God's Word presents to us. What should we believe about the issues that come up as we read Scripture? Most doctrines in the Bible are fairly straightforward and obvious, but others require that we search God's Word to see what it says we should believe.

In this section we will be looking at six biblical doctrines that often mystify Christians and non-Christians alike. These doctrines deal with some of the most serious issues in Christianity: evil and suffering, sin, hell, Satan, the Trinity, and universalism. Some of these doctrines have caused people to leave the Christian faith or refuse to even consider it. They need to be taken very seriously and answered with compassion, clarity and care.

The proper understanding of these controversial issues can lead to a life of depth and confidence. As we look at some of the more divisive issues, I will outline both sides of the debate and leave the conclusion to the reader. Not all Christians agree on these questions, so sometimes we must agree to disagree about topics that are not fully explained in God's Word. The key issue is whether we are willing to study God's Word carefully and ask him to guide us into the truth. Our understanding of some questions will no doubt grow as we mature in our Christian walk, learn more about Scripture and receive further instruction in our belief system from pastors, teachers and fellow Christians. Let's together open our minds and hearts to God's Word and see where these six questions lead us.

5

If God Is Good and All-Powerful, Why Is There Evil and Suffering in the World?

Heather, a young woman in my college religion class, went through a terrible experience right before the class started. Her parents had died long ago and she was raised by a loving grandfather. He was a very good man, a Christian, and she loved him very much. But he had a massive heart attack and died just before the course began. In that class I brought in speakers from dozens of religions, and the students asked them questions about their faith. Heather asked each of the presenters the same question, "Why would God let a good man like my grandfather die and leave me alone when he could have healed him if he wanted to?" Whether the person was an evangelical pastor, a Catholic priest, a Muslim imam or a New Age guru, their answers never satisfied her.

TED TURNER'S QUESTION

This is a question all of us must face. Ted Turner, of Turner Broadcasting System, referred to the problem of evil in his acceptance speech for the honor of being named "Humanist of the Year" by the American Humanist Association in 1990. He shared that when his fifteen-year-old sister became ill, he, a young Christian at the time, stayed up all night praying for her healing. In the morning she was dead. Turner announced that at that moment he stopped believing in God and became a humanist. This kind of crisis has caused many people to reject the Christian faith.

Theologians from every religion have dealt with this question for centuries. The question, If God is good and all-powerful, why is there evil and suffering in the world? has two parts. (1) If God allows evil and suffering even though he could stop them, then he is not good. And (2) if God cannot stop evil and suffering, then he is not all-powerful. These assertions have turned many people against Christianity for life.

THE THEODICY QUESTION

The experience of evil and suffering either draws people closer to God or pushes them farther away from him. An entire area of Christian theology is related to justifying the ways of God in the face of evil. This is called "theodicy." This is not an easy issue, and it cannot be answered quickly or simply. Thousands of books have been written on this subject. When Heather asked me the same question the last day of class, I shared her grief and then tried to answer her question.

1. We need to ask a preliminary question before we can deal with the main one, and that is, where do evil and suffering come from? First, we know that according to the book of Genesis evil entered the world through the work of Satan, the serpent (see Genesis 3; Revelation 12:9). He tempted Adam and Eve to disobey God and do what God had commanded them not to do. When they fell into sin, evil entered human experience. But couldn't God have avoided that by making Adam and Eve and their children incapable of sinning? Yes, he could, but then we wouldn't be full human beings. We either would be amoral robots, unable to decide things for ourselves, or we would live with God constantly intervening to stop us from doing anything that might be wrong. In the first case we could neither choose to love or hate God, to obey or defy God, to do good or evil, or to love or hate others. Amoral robots do not represent true humanity. They represent a humanity stripped of all values, principles and personal decision making. The same people who accuse God of ruining things by allowing evil would be the first to shout foul at the thought of God making us amoral robots.

Let's look at the second case. If God intervened in our lives to stop us from doing anything wrong, what would our lives be like?

A student wakes up in the morning and realizes that she is going to be late for school, so she jumps into her car with the intent to speed, but God would zap her so she couldn't turn the key. When someone cuts her off on the highway and she intends to pass the person on the right to teach them a lesson, God would zap her again. Arriving late on the campus, she is tempted to park in the handicap zone, but zap. Finally, as she arrives in class, she would think of a lame excuse to give her professor for being late, and as she opened her mouth to say it, zap, her mouth would be paralyzed. Is there anyone who wants to live like this?

Second, suffering is shown in the Bible to be the result of personal sins, others' sins or natural causes. Since Adam and Eve's choice to sin, we live in a fallen world. A great deal of suffering is caused by our own sins or the sins of others. God made a moral universe, and there are consequences to our actions. Unfortunately, those negative consequences often reach beyond us and spill into the lives of others.

A great deal of suffering also comes from natural causes—hurricanes, tsunamis, fires, floods, tornadoes and so on. Everyone without exception is exposed to these dangers. Some have asked me, "But couldn't God protect Christians from those things?" Well, he could, but what would be the result? Our non-Christian friends, relatives and neighbors would watch as they and their families went through terrible suffering while the Christians around them had no problems at all. "Yes, but wouldn't that make them want to be Christians too?" another student asks. Yes, but Christians for what reason? Would they seek God because they recognized their sin and guilt before a holy God and wanted to enter into a loving relationship with him, or would they seek God to avoid suffering? God, in his wisdom, has allowed Christians to suffer so we can show the world how to suffer victoriously! We "pass through the waters" (Isaiah 43:2) just like everyone else does, but God goes through them with us and gives us victory and a powerful testimony of trust and love that the world cannot easily deny.

My mother died of cancer in her early sixties. I came back from Colombia, South America, where I was working as a missionary, to be with her as she suffered her last days in the hospital. One day, as my family and I were visiting her, we began to crack jokes and laugh like crazy people. Hearing us, one of the nurses cornered me later and said, "Do you people know how serious your mother's condition is? Do you know she is going to die?" I assured her that we all knew that unless the Lord intervened, she would die. "Then why do you laugh so much?" I explained that since the Lord Jesus had come into our lives, we had experienced tremendous joy as a family, and although we would be saddened by her death and would miss her, we knew that we would be with her forever in heaven. "So we are happy, though sad." She just shook her head and walked out of the room.

My mother died, and on the day of her funeral, as I stepped into the pulpit to preach her "coronation sermon," I noticed that nurse sitting in the front row. After the service I went up to her and said, "It's wonderful to see you here, but do you always attend your patients' funerals?" She said, "No, I never do, but this was different. Many people have tried to witness to me about Christ throughout my life and I resisted them, but when I saw your mother with such joy in spite of the terrible pain she was suffering, I couldn't resist anymore. I gave my life to Christ." My mother's ability to withstand suffering with victory, hope and joy was used by God to bring a nurse to faith in him! That is God's plan for his children who suffer.

2. So, why does God allow evil and suffering in the world? God allows evil and suffering because the alternative is worse. When God created us, he had a choice: create us without free will in order to avoid evil and suffering, or create us with free will and use the evil and suffering to perfect us. God chose plan B. Why? Because he loves us too much to take away our ability to choose to love and obey him and help others. But that ability has a dark side. If I can choose to love, I can also choose to hate. If I can choose to obey, I can also choose to disobey. If I can choose to love and help others, I can also choose to hate and harm others. It is a total package that cannot be unraveled. He could either create robots or free moral agents. In his love, God decided to give us free will so that we could be fully human and choose to be in a loving relationship with him and others. No one that I know would want the alternative world. Such a world has been depicted so poignantly in many science fiction works—a world in which everyone is controlled, programmed and devoid of real humanity. God is willing to risk the results of free choice and personal suffering to save us from that kind of world.

In short, God loves us too much to remove the possibility of evil and suffering from our lives because he would also have to remove free will and our full humanity. The Bible also makes it clear that God calls people to faith by letting them see the negative consequences of the evil in their lives (see Romans 1–2). God's Word also promises that suffering helps us stay humble and allows us to show the world that the power in our lives is not ours but God's. The apostle Paul went to God three times asking him to remove the "thorn" in his flesh, but God did not do that. Rather, he said to Paul, "My grace is sufficient for you, for [My] power is perfected in [your] weakness." Paul's response was, "when I am weak, then I am strong" (2 Corinthians 12:9-10). That is the true Christian response to suffering!

PRAYING THE PRINCIPLE

Lord, thank you for allowing me to choose. Help me to choose life, blessing and the good so that I can bring glory to You and live a life full of purpose and joy.

> I call heaven and earth to witness against you today, that I have set before you life and death, the blessing and the curse. So choose life in order that you may live, you and your descendants. (Deuteronomy 30:19)

DISCUSSING THE PRINCIPLE

1. How did Ted Turner lose his Christian faith? Why?

2. What are the two assertions that often accompany the title question of this chapter? Why are they so devastating to people's faith? Have you struggled with this question? Explain.

3. Where do evil and suffering come from, and why didn't God choose to make a different world?

4. In what sense is suffering the result of personal sin and natural causes? Couldn't God avoid that result?

5. How did the suffering of the author's mother bring a blessing to someone else? Explain.

6. Why does God allow evil and suffering in the world? What does that have to do with God's love for us? Have you settled this issue in your heart in spite of the sufferings you have experienced?

6

What Is Sin, and Why Is It Such a Big Deal to God?

The nature of sin is one of those questions often asked by students the last day of a course when I open up to them about what I believe. It has been asked in many different forms, but a young woman named Dawn got right to the point. "Dr. Hundley, why is sin such a big deal? Why does God get so upset about it?" This is one of those million-dollar questions that are very difficult to answer quickly. I answered Dawn briefly, but I began to incorporate the more complete answer into my lectures on Judaism, which is the basis of this chapter.

THE FIRST CHAPTER OF GENESIS AND SIN

To get a handle on sin we have to go back to the first chapter of the first book in the Bible—Genesis. When God created the universe, he "saw all that He had made, and behold, it was *very good*" (Genesis 1:31, emphasis added). The word *good* is the backbone and foundation of all other beliefs in Judaism and Christianity. It is the Hebrew word *tov*, and it applies to everything in God's creation. *Tov* has a dual meaning: it is something that is according to God's will, and it is also the best for human beings. The creation illustrates that point. For example, the distance God placed between earth and the sun is exactly as he wanted it to be, and it is also the best for human beings. If earth were closer, we'd all be crispy critters. If it were farther from the sun, we would be the chosen frozen. God has made the distance between earth and the sun precisely according to his will, and that distance is the very best for human beings.

Belief in that dual meaning of *tov* is the hallmark of biblical faith. The idea that God's will is the best for us is the basis for placing our trust in him. If God's will is best, we would be foolish to violate it. If he wants the best for us, we can trust him with our lives and everything in them. However, Satan came to Eve and tried to pull those two meanings apart. He told her that if she wanted the best thing for her life, she should do the opposite of God's will. That is always Satan's ploy: do what God has said not to do—it will be good for you. He is not very creative. He still uses this trick on us today to get us to go against God's will. And often that's all it takes!

But God calls that choice *evil*. It is the Hebrew word *ra* (pronounced *raghh*—it sounds awful when you pronounce it—almost like you have something caught in your throat). Hebrew words often sound like what they mean. *Ra* too has a dual meaning: it is contrary to God's will, and it is also destructive for human beings. *Evil* means doing something that is contrary to life as God planned it. (Coincidentally, *evil* is *live* spelled backward in English.) Only self-destruction can come from going against the will of God. He created us and he knows how we function best. We disobey his will at our own peril. Sin or evil comprises those things that God knows will destroy us. He loves us so much that he wants to help us avoid them.

I have often used my watch to illustrate this point. The instructions for my watch state that it cannot be worn more than 200 feet below water. That has never been one of my personal desires, but I have perfect liberty to ignore that warning and dive down to 300 feet in the ocean. But I will also have the "privilege" of watching it explode as the pressure builds. Those who made the watch know how it functions best. If I listen to them, the watch will serve me well; if I don't, it will be destroyed.

God is like that. He made us. He knows how we best function. If we listen to him and follow his will, we will see positive results in our lives and live in satisfaction, fulfillment and blessing. If we choose to oppose God's will, we will suffer the negative consequences of frustration and self-destruction.

In the Pentateuch (the first five books of the Bible), we can easily point out those who believe this teaching and those who don't. Some people, like Joseph, trust God no matter what happens, believing that God knows what he is doing and will work out the best for Joseph's life if Joseph will trust him (even when everything seems to be going wrong). That is exactly what happened. On the other hand, Jacob rebels against God's will and suffers the consequences.

This is a fundamental decision we must make: Do we really believe that God's will is the best for us and that disobeying his will is destructive for us? That one decision is the bedrock of personal faith. If we believe his will is best, we will trust him, seek him, obey him and believe in him. If we believe that violating his will is the best thing for our lives, we will distrust God, ignore him, disobey him or doubt him. We are totally free to make that choice, but the consequences are set by God. Trust leads to relationship and joy; distrust leads to separation and self-destruction. It's that simple.

HOW CAN SEX BE DESTRUCTIVE?

Inevitably, some student in my class will ask something like this, "But, Dr. Hundley, you know that the most common sin most of us students commit is sex before marriage. How could that possibly be self-destructive?" That's a good question, because it tests this teaching in a very personal way. Let's look at God's will about sex. God created sex and knows how it functions best. God wants us to wait until after the public commitment of marriage to have sex, and then enjoy it freely, with no guilt and no haunting memories.

The advantages of waiting for marriage to have sex. I have told my students that there are many advantages to waiting until they get married to have sexual intercourse, which make God's plan the best one. Here are just some:

1. No fear of sexually transmitted diseases. When we have sex with someone, we are virtually having sex with everyone our partner has ever had sex with. No premarital sex, no problem. We are now living in a time when a person can have sex with the wrong person one time and it can become a death sentence.

2. Relationships deepen and are more lasting when they are based on getting to know one another rather than seeing how fast we can get our partner into bed.

3. Controlling our sexual impulses before marriage makes it much more likely that we will be able to control them after we marry. The marriage ceremony does not usually change the attitudes, commitments and drives we had before marriage.

4. Discovering the joys of sex together with no fear, no guilt and no hang-ups is one of the greatest experiences in life. I have often asked my students, "What was your first sexual experience like?" For many of them, it was in the back of a car or hiding somewhere, with constant fear of discovery. God's plan is that our first sexual experience be glorious, exciting and totally free of guilt and fear. He has a great plan!

5. Something happens when you have sex with a person—something permanent. Being dumped by a lover can be a very traumatic experience that rocks our self-esteem. Divorce often results in deep emotional pain, self-doubt, depression and anger. It can leave permanent scars that make future intimate relationships, trust in others and personal confidence very challenging. When sex is involved, every breakup is like a minidivorce, with many of the same results that marital divorce produces. Those who go through a series of experiences like that are often permanently damaged by them.

God's plan wins! So, who has the best plan: Satan or God? Which plan respects the value of each person, calls for deep, long-lasting commitment and enables people to experience the joys of sex with no fear, guilt or mental roadblocks? God's plan wins out 100 percent! And if that is true for this one example of sin, it is obviously true for every other departure from God's will. Just think about how this applies to lying, cheating in school, violence, stealing, drugs or greed.

Each of those sound good and beneficial in the beginning, but each of them ends up in distrust, ignorance, counterviolence, fear, slavery to chemicals or to material things. They ruin our lives, destroying the good life that God has planned for us to live.

This is why *sin* is such a big deal to God. He made us, and he knows how our lives function best. He also knows what will rob us of the best that he has planned for us. He loves us and wants the best for our lives. Sin destroys us. It steals the most precious things in life and turns them into garbage. It promises instant gratification and self-fulfillment, but it delivers pain and self-destruction. If we want the best in life, we will seek God's will and do it with our whole heart.

GOD'S WILL IS BEST, NOT EASIEST

One last word: just because God's will is the *best* way to live does not mean that it is always the *easiest* way. Joseph is an excellent example. He suffered unjustly for many years, but in the end God blessed him and used his life to do great things for hundreds of thousands of people.

Likewise, the five missionaries who made the first contact with the ferocious Huaorani tribe in South America were killed by them. One of the men, Jim Elliot, wrote in his journal, "He is no fool who gives what he cannot keep to gain that which he cannot lose." Seven years later he was murdered by the Huaorani. "Wait a minute," you might say, "I thought God's will was *best*. That's awful!" But if you realize that for years those men had been bombarding heaven with prayers for the conversion of the Huaorani people, you will see their deaths in a different light. Later, some of the wives of the murdered men returned to the Huaorani village and witnessed to the people of God's love and forgiveness. Almost the entire tribe was eventually converted. I will never forget the televised scene at the Berlin Congress on Evangelism in 1964, when Elisabeth Elliot stood on the platform and a Huaorani chief entered the stage holding a spear in his hand. He handed her the spear and said, "This is the spear I used to kill your husband. I don't need it anymore since I gave my life to Jesus. Please forgive me." They embraced, and the vision that those five men had for the Huaorani coming to faith in Christ was fulfilled in that moment. So, God's will is not always easy, but it is always best. We all have to die; the question is what your life will count for: eternity or self-seeking pleasure. I would rather die in the center of God's will than live in the whirlpool of sins that drag me down into eternal destruction. Wouldn't you?

Sins are actions contrary to God's will because they destroy our lives and rob us of the joy, satisfaction and fulfillment that God wants us to have in this life. God's will is always best, even when it isn't easy or successful according to normal human standards. Living in God's will brings abundant, victorious, overcoming life, but giving in to evil and sin brings personal destruction, frustration and failure. That's why sin is so serious to God—he loves us and wants the *best* for our lives![1]

PRAYING THE PRINCIPLE

Lord, I trust you with my life. I believe that you want the best for me—not the easiest but the best! And I gladly submit my life to your will, knowing that sins are those things that you have determined will hurt me and thwart your excellent plan for my life. Help me to run from sin like I would from a poisonous snake, and help me to run straight into your arms of love!

> "I know the plans that I have for you," declares the LORD, "plans for welfare and not for calamity to give you a future and a hope. Then you will call upon Me and come and pray to Me, and I will listen to you. You will seek Me and find *Me* when you search for Me with all your heart." (Jeremiah 29:11-13)

DISCUSSING THE PRINCIPLE

1. What do the words *tov* and *ra* mean, and why is their dual meaning "the hallmark of biblical faith"?

2. How does the author's watch illustration apply to our view of good and evil?

3. What is the "fundamental decision" we must all make about God's will?

4. So why is sin such a "big deal" to God?

5. What does it mean to say that God's will is the best, but it is not always the easiest way to live?

6. How has this chapter helped you see the wisdom of avoiding sin and doing God's will?

7

Is Hell a Literal Place of Burning Torture, and Who Goes There?

Ken came to my office with a very serious look on his face. His question was, "Dr. Hundley, how can a loving God torture people for all eternity in a burning hell?" Many Christians (and multitudes of non-Christians) share this concern. It is almost inconceivable to many people that a merciful God could possibly condemn millions of people to eternal torture in a fiery hell.

Del is a good friend who teaches a Sunday school class in our local church. He often complains that there is not enough preaching and teaching on hell in the modern church. He mentions this so often that I sometimes refer to him jokingly as *Give 'em hell, Del!* But seriously, he has a valid point. The doctrine of hell is important for Christians, and it is crucial that we know what we do and don't believe about it. Let's try to shed some light on this controversial subject.

THE IMPORTANCE OF THE DOCTRINE OF HELL

1. There are valid reasons why it is crucially important to teach the doctrine of hell in the church. First, it is a question of the authority of God's Word. Either you believe in the entire Bible or you don't. No one has the right to pick and choose what they will accept from

God's Word, and hell is definitely there. *Second, the doctrine of hell is a litmus test for many kinds of cults.* Whether we are talking about Scientology, Metaphysical Christianity, Christian Science or New Age religions, they all deny the reality of hell and therefore the authority of God's Word. *Third, the doctrine of hell reminds us that we live in a moral universe, created by God, in which bad choices bring negative consequences.* Hell is a reminder that no one ultimately gets away with sin. Someone always pays for our sins—either we pay for them ourselves in eternal separation from God, or Jesus pays for them on the cross. *Fourth, this doctrine also helps us see to what extent God is a gentleman.* He will not force fellowship on anyone. Those who refuse to have a relationship with him during their lifetime will find God respecting their decision for all eternity. This truth is especially important in light of the idea that God is a cruel, heartless, vindictive ogre who delights in seeing people consigned to hell for all eternity. C. S. Lewis makes the point masterfully in his book *The Great Divorce*: people make their own choice, for a variety of reasons, to refuse heaven and choose hell. God respects their decision. *Fifth, the doctrine of hell reminds us that the end of those who live self-sufficient lives without submitting to God is eternal separation from God and everything good.*

2. Many of our ideas of hell come from our cultural upbringing, which is based largely on Dante's Divine Comedy *and paintings we have seen, rather than on the teachings of the Bible.* In the *Divine Comedy*, Dante describes hell as a physical place of torture and pain. His seven circles of hell reveal Dante's view of how God will punish people who have committed various sins. His portrayal of gruesome tortures being inflicted on the damned by frightening demons is all some people know about hell. Complicating the problem, artists like Domenico di Michelino have illustrated Dante's vision of the inferno in powerful paintings, giving people a visual picture of what Dante wrote. These medieval images have permeated our culture and have led many of us to picture hell as a place full of red demons with forked tails and horns roasting their screaming victims over roaring fires. Needless to say, Dante's concept of hell does not line up with the teaching of the Bible on this subject.

3. *The New Testament is very clear about who will end up in hell.* In Matthew 11:20-24, Jesus describes those who refuse to repent and receive the gospel as being condemned to hell. In Matthew 13:49-50, Jesus teaches that the wicked will be sent to hell. In Luke 16:19-31, Jesus tells the parable of the rich man who refuses to repent and is sent to Hades. Jesus warns in John 5:28-29 that those who do evil deeds will come forth from their tombs to a resurrection of judgment. In 2 Thessalonians 1:5-9, Paul writes of those who "do not know God and . . . do not obey the gospel of our Lord Jesus." He says they "will pay the penalty of eternal destruction, away from the presence of the Lord and from the glory of His power." Later in the same epistle Paul maintains that "those who did not receive the love of the truth so as to be saved" and "took pleasure in wickedness" will be judged and will perish without hope (2 Thessalonians 2:10-12). In Revelation, John writes that those who worship "the beast" will be "tormented with fire and brimstone" (Revelation 14:9-11). At the end of that book John asserts that those whose names were "not found written in the book of life" were "thrown into the lake of fire" (Revelation 20:11-15). It is clear that the deciding factor for whether a person goes to hell is repentance, obedience to the gospel and salvation through belief in Jesus Christ. Those who do not meet those requirements are separated from God for all eternity. However, these passages also make it obvious that they are sent to hell because of their own choice to resist God and his truth, not out of some vindictive, hateful explosion of rage on God's part.

4. *Probably the most repeated question Christians (and non-Christians) have about hell is, "Is it a physical place of burning torture?"* To answer that question, it is necessary to decide whether the passages that describe hell are similes, metaphors or straightforward descriptions. Are they factual accounts or imaginative visions? Sincere Christians differ on these questions. Some would say that the descriptions of hell are like Jesus saying, "I am the door," which is a metaphor that

should not be taken literally. Likewise, when Jesus says that the kingdom of God is like a mustard seed, that simile should not be taken literally. Some Christians point out that many of the descriptions of hell occur in parables and visions, which are not to be interpreted in a literal sense. Added to this is the fact that many of the references to hell in the New Testament use the Greek form of the Hebrew word *Gehenna*. In the Old Testament, *Gehenna* was a valley south of Jerusalem where pagan worship ceremonies were performed. In Jesus' day, *Gehenna* had become a garbage heap where the people of Jerusalem threw their trash. This pile of garbage burned day and night, leading many Christian interpreters to believe that the use of this term for a burning hell is figurative, not literal.

Hell is spiritual, not physical. Many sincere Christians who believe hell is a spiritual, not a physical, reality emphasize Paul's extensive description of the afterlife in 1 Corinthians 15. In this passage Paul is writing mainly about heaven, but it seems reasonable to assume that hell and heaven are the same kind of spiritual realities. That is, if heaven is spiritual and not physical, then hell must be a spiritual state and not a physical one as well. For those Christians, Paul is saying that (1) there are heavenly bodies and there are earthly bodies (v. 40); (2) in the resurrection of the dead, a human being's body is "sown a natural body, it is raised a spiritual body" (v. 44); (3) flesh and blood cannot inherit the kingdom of God (v. 50); and (4) the perishable cannot inherit the imperishable (v. 50). This passage seems to indicate that our bodies in the afterlife are not like earthly bodies; they are spiritual, imperishable and heavenly. Now, if our bodies after death become "spiritual bodies" rather than flesh and blood, it seems logical to many Christians that heaven and hell are spiritual states, not physical ones too.

Those who believe hell is a physical place of torture. Other equally sincere Christians point out that many of the descriptions of hell in the New Testament use the term *Hades*, not *Gehenna*, avoiding the tendency to see them as figurative rather than literal.[1] Most of the passages are neither parables nor visions, similes or metaphors, but literal passages in which Jesus describes what hell is like. They would emphasize the many times hell is described as a place of fiery punishment (such as Matthew 5:22; 13:40-42; Mark 9:45-47). Those Christians believe that these are very literal descriptions of what hell is like, and they hold that these descriptions should be taken seriously: hell is a physical place of fire and punishment.

Both groups believe they are being submissive to the authority of God's Word and are seeking to interpret it faithfully, but they disagree with each other on this point. To further muddy the waters, we must also note that Jesus' resurrected body was neither totally spiritual nor totally physical. He could pass through walls, but he could also eat fish with his disciples.

Agreeing to disagree. My wife and I have been talking about this during the forty-some years of our marriage, and we have not come to full agreement about it. I could be wrong, and she could be right (or vice versa!). I don't think there is enough unequivocal biblical evidence to decide the question with absolute certainty. In this controversial issue we might do well to follow John Wesley's sage advice: "Agree to disagree; but resolve to love." My wife and I have certainly practiced that counsel! Ultimately, whatever hell is like, I don't want to be there, and I assume no one else does either, if they believe in it, and they should.

PRAYING THE PRINCIPLE

Lord, hell is terrible, frightening, horrifying and hopeless. I don't want to see anyone I know go there. Please help me today to be a more loving, understanding, sensitive and Spirit-empowered witness to them so that will never happen.

> After all it is only just for God to repay with affliction those who afflict you, and *to give* relief to you who are afflicted and to us as well when the Lord Jesus will be revealed from heaven with His mighty angels in flaming fire, dealing out retribution to those who do not know God and to those who do not obey the gospel

of our Lord Jesus. These will pay the penalty of eternal destruction, away from the presence of the Lord and from the glory of His power. (2 Thessalonians 1:6-9)

DISCUSSING THE PRINCIPLE

1. What are the five reasons given for why it is so important to teach the doctrine of hell?

2. According to the New Testament, who is sent to hell and why?

3. Why do some Christians believe that the descriptions of hell in the New Testament are metaphorical or symbolic, not literal and physical?

4. How does Paul's teaching in 1 Corinthians 15 bolster the argument of those who believe hell is spiritual, not physical?

5. What do those who see hell as a physical place of punishment say about Paul's teaching in 1 Corinthians 15?

6. How does the principle "agree to disagree" apply to this discussion? Where do you stand on this question?

8

Why Did God Create Satan?

Sheila had been struggling with a series of problems—her son was going through terrible depression, her father had just died, her body was wracked with pain from back injuries, and her church was going through some serious problems. As she looked at what was happening around her, she concluded that much of it was the direct work of Satan to destroy lives. "Why did God create Satan, anyway?" she asked. "He tries to spoil everything!"

This is not the kind of question that can be answered in thirty seconds, so I asked if she and her husband would go out to eat with my wife and me to talk about it. She agreed, and we went to a restaurant and talked it out. I didn't really feel prepared to answer her question thoroughly, but, as is often the case, afterward I was able to think it through more and look at the Scriptures and come up with the following explanation.

WHY GOD CREATED SATAN

1. We often attribute things to Satan that he is not actually responsible for. We live in a fallen world in which many harmful things take place simply because people do wrong things. When people make bad decisions, often there are consequences for those around them. Although Satan may sometimes influence people to do these things and rejoices in them, he doesn't necessarily cause them directly. The famous comic line "The devil made me do it" was funny because we all knew that the person who said it was responsible, and now, caught in the act, wanted to shift the blame to the devil. Attributing too much to Satan ignores human responsibility and gives him more credit than he deserves.

2. **When God created Satan, he was not the evil spirit he is now.** Satan was a brilliant angel in God's presence. He served God and had the pure nature of an angel. But because of his excessive pride and his desire to be equal to God, he and the angels supporting him rebelled, waged war against God and were cast out of heaven. Since then, Satan has done everything he can to thwart God's purposes and corrupt humanity. Although he is now a despicable spirit full of hate, lies, seduction and evil, he did not start out that way (see Job 1:1-12; Isaiah 14:12-15; Luke 10:18; 2 Peter 2:4; Jude 6; Revelation 12:7-12).

3. **God knew how Satan would turn out, but created Satan anyway to test our obedience and trust in God in the face of temptation and undeserved suffering.** God knows everything from the beginning to the end of history as if it were present tense. He knew full well what Satan would do when he created him, but he created him anyway because

- *God will not violate anyone's free will—not even Satan's.* The free will of his created beings is such a precious thing to God that he will not violate it, even when he foreknows the future negative consequences that will arise. If God chose to prevent his people from doing evil by not allowing them to be born, none of us would exist. The same holds true for Satan. God refused to deprive him of free will even though he knew the future consequences of his rebellion.

- *God uses Satan to test our obedience to God.* Adam and Eve lived in a perfect paradise, fellowshiping with God and enjoying life. But God allowed Satan to tempt Adam and Eve in order to test their obedience to God's command not to eat of the tree of the knowledge of good and evil (Genesis 3:1-24). They failed the test, and God punished them for their disobedience, but he also continued to love and care for them. He established the principle that his will is best for human beings, which was proved over and over again in the Old Testament. Without Satan's temptation and the first couple's rebellious eating of the fruit of the tree of the knowledge of good and evil, Adam and Eve would never have entered that deeper relationship with God based on free choice and personal experience of the consequences of choosing evil instead of the good life God wanted for them. Scripture teaches us that there are destructive consequences to sin, and sometimes people are "delivered to Satan" to learn that hard lesson and consequently repent and return to God (see 1 Corinthians 5:5).

- *God also uses Satan to test our trust in God in the face of undeserved suffering.* The book of Job is an excellent example of how God allows Satan to test our trust in God through undeserved suffering. Now, there is such a thing as *deserved suffering* (see 1 Peter 4:12-16). We sometimes bring suffering on ourselves. A friend shared this conversation with his doctor: "Doctor, why do I get out of breath when I climb a flight of stairs?" The doctor responded, "Because you eat too much, don't exercise enough, and you are fat!" Often, we suffer much more serious effects from the wrong choices we make in life. The proper response to deserved suffering is repenting, accepting the consequences and making changes if they are possible.

  But the book of Job describes *undeserved suffering.* Job was a good man, blameless, upright and God-fearing. God asks Satan, "Have you considered My servant Job? For there is no one like him on the earth, a blameless and upright man, fearing God and turning away from evil" (Job 1:8). Satan counters that Job is upright, blameless and God-fearing only because God has protected him from suffering. He argues that if Job had to suffer, he would curse God instead of trusting him. God allows Satan to afflict Job, within certain limits, and Satan does so. But Job remains true to his trust in God. He utters those famous words, "Though He slay me, / I will hope [trust] in Him" (Job 13:15). This tremendous declaration of faith could only come from the lips of someone who has experienced undeserved suffering but still trusts in God. When Satan brings undeserved suffering into our lives, it is an excellent opportunity to show our trust in God in spite of our circumstances. It's easy to say we trust God when things are good, but deep trust in him can only show itself when we go through difficult times and still praise and trust God in spite of them.

THE ATTITUDE THAT PLEASES GOD

A dear lady in our Sunday school class shared recently that she had just been diagnosed with breast cancer. She said, "If God wants to heal me, that's fine, and if he doesn't, I will go to be with him and that's fine too." That's the kind of trust God is looking for in us. It pleases him, is a tremendous witness and gives our lives a rock-solid foundation that nothing can shake. Joyce Meyer says, "We will always face obstacles and difficulties. . . . We would be wise to settle down and deal with the challenges He puts before us. Whatever they are, if we will receive them as his training for us and submit to his will, we will not get stuck, but go through to victory."[1]

So, why did God create Satan? God gave Satan a chance to be a willing, submissive servant, but Satan rebelled and rejected God's will, becoming a hateful, seductive spirit bent on destroying human beings. But in an incredible display of his power and sovereignty, God has found ways to use Satan's attacks to perfect us, test us and lead us into a deeper life of trust and praise than we could have known without those attacks. Getting back to our friend Sheila, her son worked through his depression and became stronger as a result of it. He battled it again later on, but did much better that time. Her father's victorious passing into heaven inspired many people in their faith in the Lord as he died with absolute confidence in his heavenly home and the love of his Savior. Sheila still struggles with pain, but, as she told me recently, God has given her the grace to put up with it and even use it as a means for witness. The problems in her church brought many members to a place of repentance and wholehearted seeking after God that has made their spiritual walk deeper and more powerful than ever. God's Word says, "God causes all things to work together for good to those who love God, to those who are called according to His purpose" (Romans 8:28). When it says "all things," it means *all things*—even the attacks of Satan. God created Satan ultimately for our good.

PRAYING THE PRINCIPLE

Lord, thank you that even Satan's attacks can be used by you in my life to perfect, confirm, strengthen and establish me. Help me to resist him, firm in my faith in you, and seek your help so that Satan has to flee from me and leave me alone—until the next time.

> Be of sober *spirit*, be on the alert. Your adversary, the devil, prowls around like a roaring lion, seeking someone to devour. But resist him, firm in *your* faith, knowing that the same experiences of suffering are being accomplished by your brethren who are in the world. After you have suffered for a little while, the God of all grace, who called you to His eternal glory in Christ, will Himself perfect, confirm, strengthen *and* establish you. (1 Peter 5:8-10)

DISCUSSING THE PRINCIPLE

1. In what way do people sometimes attribute actions to Satan which he is not really responsible for?

2. What was Satan like when God first created him, and how has he changed? Why?

3. Since God knew what Satan would do in the future, why did he allow him to be created?

4. How does God use Satan to test our obedience to him?

5. How does God use Satan to test our trust in him when we go through undeserved suffering? Has he done that in your life? Did it work?

6. What is the trust attitude that pleases God? Why is it so important?

9

Can We Understand the Trinity?

Julie, a first-year student in my world religions class, was trying to decide whether to follow the Christian religious tradition of her family or adopt a different religious understanding—possibly Buddhism. As I taught on the doctrine of God in Christianity, I mentioned the Trinity. Julie immediately raised her hand and said, "I don't get it. How can God be three persons and still be one person? That doesn't make sense—either God is one or there are three Gods." I thanked Julie for giving me such an excellent segue into my lecture on the Trinity. I jokingly asked her to please come to all of my classes!

The doctrine of the Trinity is without a doubt the most difficult doctrine in Christianity. One of the problems is that the word *Trinity* does not appear in the Bible. It is an invented word used to describe biblical evidence and tie together several different biblical concepts. The Bible simply refers to God as Father, Son and Holy Spirit, but it never bothers to flesh out how that can be.

BIBLICAL REFERENCES TO THE TRINITY

There are several passages in which all three divine persons are mentioned together. For example, when Jesus' birth is announced to Mary, all three persons of the Trinity are mentioned: "The *Holy Spirit* will come upon you, and the power of the *Most High* [God—see v. 32] will overshadow you; and for that reason, the holy Child shall be called the *Son of God*" (Luke 1:35, emphasis added). At Jesus' baptism the text records that Jesus, *the Son*, is baptized by John; then the *Spirit* descends on Jesus like a dove, and the *Father* says, "This is My beloved *Son*, in whom I am well-pleased" (Matthew 3:16-17, emphasis added). In John 14:16-17, Jesus, the *Son*, promises his disciples that he will ask the *Father* to send them the *Spirit* after he is gone. Significantly, Jesus mentions all three members of the Trinity in his final charge to his disciples to go and "make disciples of all the nations, baptizing them in the name of the *Father* and the *Son* and the *Holy Spirit*" (Matthew 28:19, emphasis added). These, and other similar passages, make it clear that the idea of the Trinity is repeatedly described in the New Testament, without ever bringing it all together into one single doctrinal expression or term.

Throughout the history of the Christian church there have been many attempts to explain or illustrate the doctrine of the Trinity. During the period in which Greek thought dominated, intricate Greek philosophical terms were used to carefully portray the differences and equalities between God the Father, Son and Holy Spirit. Many analogies have been used to describe the Trinity. The egg has been used to illustrate three in one: shell, yolk and white. Human relations have also been used. I am a father, a son and a husband, but I am one person—three in one. Water has also been utilized as an analogy. H_2O can be liquid, vapor or ice, but it is still H_2O—three in one. One math professor told me to explain to my students that the Trinity cannot be described mathematically as $1 + 1 + 1 = 3$, but as $1 \times 1 \times 1 = 1$. I like that.

NO SPATIAL DIFFERENTIATION BETWEEN MEMBERS OF THE TRINITY

All of these analogies are helpful, but they don't really get to the point. The fact is, God is a Spirit and there is no physical differentiation between the three persons of the Trinity. It is almost impossible to wrap our finite minds around the idea that God is not physical. You can't say, "The Father is over there, and the Son is over here, and the Spirit is somewhere else." They have no physical location. They are everywhere at the same time, but not in a physical sense. As Jesus said, "God is Spirit" (John 4:24). God is a Spirit being. He can manifest himself physically, but in his person, he is not physical but spiritual.

THE TRINITY IS SPIRITUAL, NOT PHYSICAL

It is almost impossible for us to think of a being who is not physical. We think in spatial terms about almost everything, even things that are not physical. We say that we have love in our hearts, fear in our stomachs and confusion in our heads, but those states aren't really physical and they are not really located in those organs. We just talk about them that way because how else can we describe them? It is the same with the three persons of the Trinity. They are three in one and there is no spatial separation between them. The only time the Trinity ever experienced any kind of spatial division was when Jesus took on human form and lived on earth. Paul describes this event in Philippians 2:5-7 when he says, "Christ Jesus, who, although He existed in the form of God, did not regard equality with God a thing to be grasped, but emptied Himself, taking the form of a bond-servant, *and being made in the likeness of men.*" Before time, the Son existed in equality with God, but the Son emptied himself of those prerogatives in order to become a human being (John 1:1-13). During those thirty-three years, there was actual spatial separation between the Son and the Father and Holy Spirit, even though there was still spiritual union between them. But as soon as Jesus ascended, he returned right back to his former state as a spirit, an equal part of the Trinity, which he had enjoyed throughout eternity before his birth and is enjoying for eternity since his ascension (see John 1:1; 17:5; Mark 16:19; Acts 7:55-56; Hebrews 4:14-15).

GOD IS UNFATHOMABLE

God is indescribable, unfathomable and incomprehensible. He is different from us, not just in his superiority to us, but he is a totally different kind of being than we are. We are physical beings; he is a spirit being. We are in time; he is in eternity. We have a spatial location; he has no location. We can be seen; he is invisible. We are finite; he is infinite. It's no wonder that our limited, finite, physically oriented minds have so much trouble understanding who he is and how he exists as he does as one God in three persons. When we try to understand God, we are like ants trying to understand mathematical multiplication. It just isn't going to compute!

Does that make God any less accessible or intelligible? No, because in his graciousness God has revealed himself to us in his Word, in Jesus and in our own relationship with him. We know all we need to know to be able to love, obey, worship, praise and reverence him. Though we are never able to fully comprehend the Trinity, it will not matter one bit when we stand in his presence some day and experience his glory, majesty, perfection, love and power! As Reginald Heber's hymn says,

Holy, holy, holy! Lord God Almighty!
Early in the morning our song shall rise to Thee;
Holy, holy, holy; merciful and mighty!
God in three Persons, blessed Trinity![1]

Some day, we will be in his immediate presence, and we will praise the triune God forever and ever!

PRAYING THE PRINCIPLE

Holy Trinity—Father, Son and Holy Spirit—I praise you for your oneness, your unity, your harmony and your love. You are a model of community and loving fellowship. Help me to imitate you and reproduce your character and mutuality in my relationships with all those who love you, to the praise of your glory.

Believe Me that I [Jesus] am in the Father and the Father is in Me. . . .

I will ask the Father and he will give you another Helper, that He may be with you forever; *that is* the Spirit of truth, whom the world cannot receive, because it does not see Him or know Him, *but* you know Him because He abides with you and will be in you. (John 14:11, 16-17)

DISCUSSING THE PRINCIPLE

1. Name three New Testament passages in which the Father, Son and Holy Spirit are named together.

2. What are four common analogies used to describe the Trinity? Are any of those helpful to you?

3. Why is it so hard for us to picture a "spiritual being" like God and understand that there is no physical separation between the members of the Trinity? Do you have trouble with that?

4. What is the only event that has ever produced spatial division between the members of the Trinity? Why do you think that was necessary?

5. Name some of the essential differences between the kind of being God is and the kind we are. Do those differences make God inaccessible to us? Why not?

6. Will you ever be able to understand the doctrine of the Trinity completely? In what ways are we able to respond to God and his self-revelation? Is that enough for you?

10

Will Everyone
Be Saved in the End?

Cheryl, one of the adults in our Sunday school class, met a lady who attends a Unity church. They struck up a conversation, and Cheryl's friend shared that her church believes that everyone will be saved in the end and that there is no hell. Cheryl tried to explain her church's view, but found it difficult to get through to the friend. So Cheryl asked, "Why do some people believe that everyone will be saved?"

Universalism, as this doctrine is called, has been growing exponentially in the past few decades. In the United States the view that the greatest of virtues are tolerance and nonjudgmentalism fits in beautifully with universalism. The concept that we should never judge or condemn anyone else for their beliefs sometimes bleeds over into a conviction that God would never do that either. Hinduism and Buddhism also share this belief, as do several supposed Christian denominations like Unity Church, Unitarian Universalists, the Church of Metaphysical Christianity and many liberal Protestant groups. The idea that God is too kind and loving to condemn anyone to an eternal hell seems very comforting to many people.

ROB BELL'S *LOVE WINS* AND ITS PROMOTION OF UNIVERSALISM

Rob Bell founded Mars Hill Bible Church in Grandville, Michigan, which now has an average Sunday attendance of ten thousand people.

He has published seven books and was chosen as one of *Time* magazine's 2011 "most influential people in the world." His book *Love Wins* has caused a great deal of controversy among evangelicals who see it as a denial of the biblical doctrine of hell and a blatant espousal of universalism.

Bell's book begins with this very clear statement:

> It's been clearly communicated to many that this belief [that Christians will spend eternity in heaven, while the rest of humanity will spend it in hell] is a central truth of the Christian faith and to reject it is, in essence, to reject Jesus. This is misguided and toxic and ultimately subverts the contagious spread of Jesus' message of love, peace, forgiveness, and joy that our world desperately needs to hear. And so this book.[1]

The book contains five central arguments in favor of universalism, which we will consider now.

1. It cannot be true, says Bell, that "God created millions of people over tens of thousands of years who are going to spend eternity in anguish."[2] Actually, it is true. Jesus, the Savior, said, "The gate is small and the way is narrow that leads to life, and there are few who find it" (Matthew 7:14). Was Jesus mistaken? Was he being cruel and heartless, or just realistic? Was he misguided and toxic, subverting his own message? The fact is that most people take the way "that leads to destruction" in spite of the fact that God has sent his own Son to die in their place and pay the price for their sins so they can find forgiveness, peace and salvation. God has given us a chance to be saved. We can accept or reject it. Sadly, most people reject it.

2. According to Bell, it is not true that if a person has a "personal relationship with God through Jesus" they will be saved from hell and judgment. Bell goes on to affirm that "the phrase 'personal relationship' is found nowhere in the Bible," so it cannot possibly be "the heart of the Christian faith."[3] Although "personal relationship" does not appear in Scripture (just as *Trinity* doesn't), it is a way of describing what does appear throughout the Old and New Testaments: knowing

and loving God. The Hebrew verb "know" (*yada*) occurs more than one thousand times in the Old Testament, and more than twenty of those passages describe knowing God personally. The Greek verb "know" (*ginōskō*) appears more than two hundred times in the New Testament, and more than twenty-five of those describe knowing God in a personal way. Knowing God expresses a personal relationship with him!

The Hebrew verb "love" (*aheb*) is used almost three hundred times in the Old Testament. Of those passages, almost thirty refer to people's love for God. The Greek verb "love" (*agapaō*) appears over one hundred times in the New Testament, and is used almost twenty of those times to denote loving God. *Loving God describes a personal relationship with him!* The use of "personal relationship" is just a shorthand way of describing *knowing and loving God*, and that personal relationship of knowing God and loving him is the central truth of Scripture.

3. Heaven is not a state separate from the world, says Bell; heaven is this earth changed to conform to God's will. When we help people with their physical problems, we, in effect, bring heaven to earth.[4] Bell states, "Jesus invites us, in this life, in this broken, beautiful world, to experience the life of heaven now."[5] This is the classic liberal approach to social work as the means for bringing God's kingdom to earth. It eliminates any real concern about being in heaven after death, and substitutes social activism as the best way to change the world and bring heaven into people's lives now. Although evangelicals do not reject the need to minister to the physical needs of people (in my travels around the world I have seen many more evangelical hospitals, orphanages, clinics, schools, leprosariums and feeding programs than liberal ones), we insist that spiritual ministry must accompany social ministry. It does little good if people are healthier, better dressed, fairly housed and well-fed as they enter eternal hell, forever separated from God and everything good. As Jesus asked, "What will it profit a man if he gains the whole world and forfeits his soul?" (Matthew 16:26).

4. Hell is not a place of eternal punishment and separation, according to Bell; it is a place of refining and pruning so that people can finally repent and be welcomed into full fellowship with God and others.[6] Bell describes his position as "the belief that, given enough time, everybody will turn to God and find themselves in the joy and peace of God's presence. The love of God will melt every hard heart, and even the most 'depraved sinners' will eventually give up their resistance and turn to God."[7] He affirms that, "At the center of the Christian tradition since the first church have been a number who insist that history is not tragic, hell is not forever, and love, in the end, wins and all will be reconciled with God," hence, the title of this book![8] Known in theology as "universal reconciliation," this view sees hell as a kind of "dry cleaner" that takes in sinners, cleans them up and sends them out renewed and redeemed. This position is clearly contrary to the plain teaching of Scripture. In the parable of the rich man and Lazarus, Jesus has Abraham tell the man in Hades: "between us and you there is a great chasm fixed, so that those who wish to come over from here to you will not be able, and *that* none may cross over from there to us" (Luke 16:26). Jesus says that those who are "accursed" will "go away into eternal punishment" (Matthew 25:46). In 2 Thessalonians 1:8-9 Paul clarifies why people are sent to hell and makes abundantly clear the eternal nature of hell: The Lord Jesus will deal "out retribution to those who do not know God and to those who do not obey the gospel of our Lord Jesus. These will pay the penalty of eternal destruction, away from the presence of the Lord and from the glory of His power." Many other passages in the New Testament teach the same thing. Hell is eternal, not temporary. It is a state of eternal separation from God, not a place for refining and improving people who have rejected God.

5. Bell says it is not necessary to accept the Christian faith to be saved. Many people find God through other religions, or no religion at all, and enter God's kingdom without ever knowing Jesus' name or the gospel story at all.[9] Bell insists that the "saving love of this par-

ticular Jesus the Christ will of course include all sorts of unexpected people from across the cultural spectrum [Muslims, Hindus, Buddhists, and Baptists from Cleveland]."[10] But what about John 14:6—"I am the way, and the truth, and the life; no one comes to the Father but through Me"? Anticipating this reaction, Bell goes to great lengths to explain his view of the meaning of the John 14 passage. He observes that Jesus makes that claim, but "what he doesn't say is how, or when, or in what manner the mechanism functions that gets people to God through him." Bell believes that this passage means that Jesus "simply claims that whatever God is doing in the world to know and redeem and love and restore the world is happening through him."[11] I have seen this many times before. Writers who are proclaiming a message that goes contrary to the church's two-thousand-year-old interpretation of a passage will go through all kinds of hermeneutical gyrations to avoid the plain meaning of the text and affirm the opposite. This is a good example. Jesus says that no one can come to the Father except through him, but Bell interprets that to mean that anyone can come to God through any means and any belief because Jesus is secretly behind all attempts to restore the world. Acts 4:12, 1 John 5:11-12 and Matthew 7:13-23 show clearly that faith in Jesus is the only way to salvation. There is no other Savior for lost humanity than Jesus, the Christ, the Son of God.

These are the closing words of Bell's book:

> Love is why I have written this book, and love is what I want to leave you with. May you experience the vast, expansive, infinite, indestructible love that has been yours all along. May you discover that this love is as wide as the sky and as small as the cracks in your heart no one else knows about. And may you know, deep in your bones, that love wins.[12]

Bell's conclusion, founded on his five unscriptural arguments, makes his universalism untenable for anyone who takes the Scripture seriously as the authoritative Word of God.

THE CHRISTIAN UNIVERSALIST ASSOCIATION

One of the more classic, established groups promoting this theology is the Christian Universalist Association. Their website explains their basic beliefs. Their doctrinal position about universalism affirms "the ultimate triumph of divine mercy and grace: that no being created will be condemned or allowed to suffer forever, but God has arranged through a benevolent plan of learning and growth for all souls to attain salvation, reconciliation, restoration, and reunion with the Source of All Being, in the fullness of the ages." The website affirms that "every person is the divine offspring of God," and that the Bible is just one text among many that offer "spiritual and moral wisdom."[13]

The website then presents a number of New Testament texts that they feel support their universalist views, among them:

(1) **John 12:32**—"And I [Jesus], if I am lifted up from the earth, will draw all men to Myself."

(2) **1 Timothy 2:4**—"[God] desires all men to be saved and to come to the knowledge of the truth."

(3) **Philippians 2:10-11**—"So that at the name of Jesus every knee will bow, of those who are in heaven and on earth and under the earth, and that every tongue will confess that Jesus Christ is Lord, to the glory of God the Father."

(4) **1 Peter 4:6**—"For the gospel has for this purpose been preached even to those who are dead, that though they are judged in the flesh as men, they may live in the spirit according to the will of God."[14]

Although at first glance, these passages may seem to make a strong case for the universalist position, we must remember that these four passages must be weighed in the light of dozens of New Testament passages that speak of judgment and hell. These four passages also must be seen in the light of three simple principles:

1. The fact that Jesus died for the whole world does not mean the whole world will be saved. Salvation is offered universally, but it must be accepted personally by those who choose to believe and give their life to God through Christ. As the author of Hebrews so beautifully says, through his death Jesus opened the way to fellowship with God (Hebrews 10:19-20). The way has been opened for all people, but people must still respond to that invitation and avail themselves of the access to God that Jesus has provided through his death on the cross. Likewise, the fact that Jesus' death draws all people to himself does not mean that they all respond to and enter into a faith relationship with him. In addition, God's desire that all people be saved expresses a portrait of God's gracious heart. It does not guarantee that all people will receive his invitation (unless, of course, you believe that everything God desires happens automatically—in which case you would have to be a universalist too).

2. *The fact that everyone will acknowledge who Jesus is when he returns to earth does not imply that everyone will be saved.* As the New Testament often records, demons acknowledged who Jesus was, but they were not saved because of it (see Mark 1:24). Jesus' power and majesty will be revealed to everyone when he returns to earth, but that is no guarantee that all who finally realize who he is will give their lives to him in submission and faith.

3. *The statement by Peter that the gospel has been preached to the dead does not imply that all dead people will have a second chance to believe in Christ (as Mormons teach).* First Peter 3:19-20 and Ephesians 4:9 state that between Jesus' death and resurrection, he went to hell and preached to the souls that were there. No text reveals what he preached to them or why he preached to them; it just says he did it. Of course, as we all know too well, preaching to someone does not guarantee a faithful response to an invitation to be saved. First Peter 3 specifically mentions these dead people as "the spirits *now* in prison, who once were disobedient, when the patience of God kept waiting in the days of Noah" (vv. 19-20). No one is sure what exactly this means. Nevertheless, the 1 Peter 3 passage does not teach that Jesus preaches to all people after they die, nor does it affirm that those to whom he preached responded in any way.

PAUL'S ANTI-UNIVERSALISM IN ROMANS 5

There is a passage in Paul's epistle to the Romans in which he could have easily argued for universalism, but he did just the opposite. In Romans 5:12-21, Paul presents the idea that sin and death came into the world through one man, Adam, and his disobedience, and spread to all of humanity. It would have seemed logical for him to say the same thing in a parallel way about Jesus' obedience effecting salvation for all people. But Paul makes it clear that that is not the case. The results of Jesus' sacrifice affect not all men but "the many" (vv. 15, 19). However, Paul insists that the justification made possible by Jesus applies to "all men" (v. 18). So, Jesus' death made it possible for all people to be justified by faith, but not all people will take advantage of that offer, only the "many."

THE DEVASTATING EFFECTS OF UNIVERSALISM

Universalism is a destructive doctrine that cuts the nerve of evangelism. It makes Jesus' sacrifice on the cross meaningless and eliminates God's judgment against sin. If universalism were true, it would mean that there is no reason to proclaim the gospel to the lost, since no one would be lost regardless of what they believe or what they do. Adolph Hitler and the apostle Paul would have ended up in the same place after death. That is untenable (unless, of course, Hitler repented and put his faith in Christ!). God is just. He punishes sin and respects people's decisions not to have fellowship with him, which he honors for all eternity. Those who think God is too loving to condemn anyone to eternal separation from him do not understand the relationship between God's love and God's holiness. He loves us all, but he hates sin and judges it in a serious, definitive way. God will not violate people's free will decision to exclude him from their lives. Those who reject him will be eternally separated from him, even as he looks on them with a tear in his eye.

PRAYING THE PRINCIPLE

Lord, I can't even think about hell without tearing up. I sincerely don't

want to see anyone go there, separated from your presence for all eternity.
Help me to remember that truth when I meet people who are lost, and
help me to witness to them about your love and your forgiveness before
it is too late.

> [God will] *give* relief to you who are afflicted and to us as well
> when the Lord Jesus will be revealed from heaven with His
> mighty angels in flaming fire, dealing out retribution to those
> who do not know God and to those who do not obey the gospel
> of our Lord Jesus. These will pay the penalty of eternal de-
> struction, away from the presence of the Lord and from the
> glory of His power. (2 Thessalonians 1:7-9)

DISCUSSING THE PRINCIPLE

1. How does universalism fit into the values of modern culture? What
   is Rob Bell's position on it?

2. Explain what you think about the four texts that the Christian Universalist Association uses to support their belief that no one will go
   to hell.

3. What are the three principles we need to keep in mind as we look
   at those passages?

4. How does Paul's teaching in Romans 5 apply to the universalism
   discussion?

5. What are some of the destructive effects of universalism?

6. If you reject universalism, how does the opposing view affect how
   you live?

PART THREE

Questions About Christian Living

What we believe as Christians naturally raises the issue of how we *act*. Practice is based on belief. We examine God's Word to see what we should believe and what we should do or not do. The Christian faith is more than just a philosophy; it is a way of life meant to be lived out according to the will of God. Our study of God's Word is not complete until it has led us to put into practice what God wills for us. An InterVarsity representative spoke in my college dorm (almost fifty years ago), and I still remember one phrase he shared with us that night: "A biblical truth is not learned until I am committed to a course of action that involves me in that truth." He was absolutely right, and I have tried to live by that principle ever since. I try to apply God's Word to my walk with him.

Our practice of the Christian life has both positive and negative sides. There are things we are instructed by God to put into practice and there are things we are instructed not to do. Two negative areas have to do with hypocrisy: (1) most Christians are hypocrites, and (2) how much sin can we get away with? Avoiding both of these errors would go a long way toward making our faith more appealing and consistent to non-Christians (and more victorious for us!). But we must also focus on positive elements of Christian practice: (1) how to study the Bible, (2) how to know God's will for our lives and (3) the place of healing in our Christian walk. These practices form the foundation of our Christian walk, so we need to consider them carefully and put them into practice with discipline, spiritual intimacy and faith. The following chapters should help us seek God in these areas and teach us to walk wisely in the center of God's will.

11

Aren't Most Christians Hypocrites?

Christians are a bunch of hypocrites. This is one of the perennial complaints of unbelievers. While at a camp, Karen, a young woman, brought this accusation to me. She was obviously weighing whether or not to throw away her Christian faith, so I asked her what had happened to bring her to that point. "It's my father. He's such a hypocrite. He's a big leader in our church, but no one knows what he's really like. He looks at porn, goes to strip clubs and drinks, but nobody in our church knows about it. They all think he's a real saint. I just can't stand it anymore." I could see how serious she was, and I counseled that she not let her father's hypocrisy rob her of her relationship with Jesus Christ. But she ended our talk insisting that she was afraid most Christians are like her father, so she wanted to leave the church.

HYPOCRISY: THE MAIN OBSTACLE TO FAITH

I am convinced, after many years of talking to people who reject the Christian faith, that this one problem is the biggest obstacle to faith for most unbelievers. They have witnessed the hypocrisy of Christians and it has turned them from the gospel. No other behavior damages more people than Christians living a lie. That's probably why Jesus was so critical of hypocrites during his ministry.

In Matthew 23, Jesus describes the essence of hypocrisy. He says that hypocrites do not practice what they preach (v. 3); they like to show off their spirituality and authority in front of others, but are sinful in secret (vv. 4-6); they "shut off the kingdom" of God from other people by their two-faced conduct (v. 13); and they are like "whitewashed tombs"—beautiful on the outside but unclean on the inside (v. 27). Jesus ends his criticism of hypocrites by warning, "You serpents, you brood of vipers, how will you escape the sentence of hell?" (v. 33). Is it any wonder that Jesus taught so much against hypocrisy?! It is so destructive, grotesque and damaging.

DEGREES OF HYPOCRISY

Now the question is—are there degrees of hypocrisy? All Christians must admit that there is some of the hypocrite in all of us. We all want to appear better than we really are. We are all on our best behavior when we're around fellow Christians. There is no one who lives up to all of the ideals of the Christian faith perfectly. We all fall short and often hide our failure by giving the appearance of being more holy than we really are. This is also true of all non-Christians. We've all known, for example, how nice a non-Christian young man was when dating a young woman, and how horribly he acted after they were married. Hypocrisy, unfortunately, is part of the universal human condition.

In Matthew 23 Jesus is condemning the extreme hypocrisy in which people put up the smokescreen of righteous conduct and belief to hide their secret sinful acts, as Karen's father did. They know full well that what they are doing is wrong, but they refuse to stop doing it, and they cover it up by faking their holy character and spirituality. When we get to that point, we are dangerously deluding ourselves and need a tremendous amount of help to face our double life and abandon it. I include myself here. That was my reality for many years. Escaping from that prison is a painful process of seeing ourselves as we really are and asking God to forgive and heal us. It is glorious when he does!

ARE CHRISTIANS HYPOCRITES?

So, are most Christians hypocrites? Well, in a sense, yes. We all try to look better than we really are. But remember, so do all non-Christians. But are most Christians hypocrites like the ones Jesus described? Thankfully, no, we are not. Although there are some exceptions, most Christians live their entire Christian lives without falling into the trap of gross sin covered up by hypocrisy. Then why do so many people think all Christians are hypocrites? Christian Colombians have a saying that *en sábana blanca se ve cada mancha* (in a white sheet you can see every spot). They mean that any failure in Christians shows up to the outside world because Christians are expected to be more morally upright and well-behaved than others are. Bad behavior that non-Christians observe in their non-Christian friends and accept without a problem causes a scandal when they see it in Christians. They don't expect Christians to act that way, and when they do, they are shocked. Just look at what the media do with problems like divorce. If a non-Christian is divorced, it's not usually a headline. But when a Christian leader gets divorced, that is big news. They expect much more of us, so they are more disillusioned when we don't measure up to their expectations. At the same time, we profess more than they do. We claim that Christ has saved and changed our lives, so when we live below the victorious life, we disappoint ourselves and scandalize the unbelieving world, giving them one more reason to reject our faith.

The Christian chorus that says "I'm just a sinner saved by grace" is absolutely true. We are not perfect. We have not arrived. Jesus loves us even when we sin, but he doesn't want to leave us there—he wants to change our lives. The extent to which we allow him to do that is the extent to which we cease giving a bad testimony with our hypocrisy.

When my wife and I were part of a youth evangelism team, each team member shared with the youth a problem, struggle or sin that we were battling in our own lives. We didn't want them to get the impression that we were perfect Christians, with no problems. We were concerned that if they placed us on too high of a pedestal, they would become discouraged when their own experience didn't match up with that ideal. I'm afraid that this kind of vulnerability and honesty is all too infrequent for Christians. This is probably why nonbelievers don't know that we openly confess we too are hypocrites. The difference is that we have sought the grace, mercy and transformation that only Christ can give to make our lives more aligned with our high ideals.

Surely one of the best ways to share Christ with unbelievers, and avoid the holier-than-thou hypocrisy trap, is to express how we struggle and how the Lord is helping us. This is especially crucial as we share our faith with our own children. This kind of testimony is much more effective than the traditional "I was saved twenty years ago and I haven't sinned since." Nobody believes that, and lying is a *sin!*

Let's be clear: the church is not a country club for the holier-than-thou crowd; it is a hospital for the sick and the needy. We don't come to church because we're good enough. We come to church asking Jesus to make us better—and he does!

PRAYING THE PRINCIPLE

Lord, I am so sorry for the years I lived in hypocrisy and falsehood. I know that my bad testimony was used by Satan to turn many people away from you. I thank you for your forgiveness and for your restoration of my life and testimony. I want to dedicate my life to bringing others to you and living a life of purity and love so that I will no longer have to be ashamed. Please help those I hurt, Lord, and bring someone across their path who will live your life with integrity and transparency and bring them back to you.

> And [Jesus] said to them, "Rightly did Isaiah prophesy of you hypocrites, as it is written:
>
> > 'THIS PEOPLE HONORS ME WITH THEIR LIPS,
> > BUT THEIR HEART IS FAR AWAY FROM ME.' " (Mark 7:6)

DISCUSSING THE PRINCIPLE

1. Why is the hypocrisy of Christians such a problem for non-Christians?

2. What are the four descriptions of hypocrites that Jesus taught in Matthew 23?

3. In what ways are all Christians somewhat hypocritical? How about non-Christians? Do you agree with the author's analysis?

4. What is the extreme form of hypocrisy that Jesus condemned in Matthew 23?

5. What is one of the best ways to avoid the holier-than-thou hypocrisy trap?

6. What is the difference between seeing the church as a country club and seeing it as a hospital?

12

How Much Can I Sin
and Still Get to Heaven?

Our college youth evangelism team was ministering in a large church in the South. As was our custom, Saturday night was dedicated to a question-and-answer time with the young people. After several questions, a young man about fourteen years old raised his hand and with a very serious look on his face asked, "How much can you sin and still get to heaven?" I'm sure my answer was not what he expected. I responded, "Why do you want to know?" and the whole group burst out laughing. With a red face, he stammered, "I was just curious." To assuage his embarrassment, I shared that all of us struggle with sin and how to live a holy and righteous life. He seemed relieved!

I went on to explain that as Christians we aren't trying to see how much sin we can get away with; we are trying to learn how to sin less. But his question is one shared by many people who wouldn't dare voice it. Many Christians want to live on the very edge of the cliff, teetering over the abyss of sin and destruction with every step. Why do so many people do this?

JAMES'S ANSWER

James says that some people are "double-minded." That is, they have one foot in the kingdom of God and the other foot in the world. They live straddling that fence, which, by the way, is extremely uncomfortable! James warns that they cannot expect to "receive anything from the Lord" (James 1:5-8).

PAUL'S ANSWER

Paul expresses grave concern about this problem in his epistles. He makes it very clear that if we live in premeditated, habitual serious sin, we will never see heaven, regardless of what we say we believe. Some of those sinners include fornicators (those engaged in premarital sex), idolaters, adulterers, effeminate (by perversion), homosexuals, thieves, the covetous, drunkards, revilers and swindlers (1 Corinthians 6:9-10). Some sins that will keep us out of heaven are "immorality, impurity, sensuality, idolatry, sorcery, enmities, strife, jealousy, outbursts of anger, disputes, dissensions, factions, envying, drunkenness, carousing" (Galatians 5:19-21). Notice that each of these sins is premeditated—we don't just fall into them. They are planned and then executed. No real Christian habitually practices these sins.

JOHN'S ANSWER

In his first epistle, John makes this clear when he asserts that "the one who practices sin is of the devil. . . . No one who is born of God practices sin" (1 John 3:8-9). Not that Christians never sin; we all do. But real Christians do not habitually live in and practice sin. There is a big difference between falling into an occasional sin and living in sin. We are all tempted every day, and we often yield to those temptations for a moment and do something we know we shouldn't. But we do not all live in sin, practice sin, premeditate sin and then carry out our plan. Those that do make it clear that they are not "born of God."

John also makes a point in his epistle to make provision for believers who *do* sin. He writes, "If we confess our sins, He is faithful and righteous to forgive us our sins and to cleanse us from all unrighteousness" (1 John 1:9). Thankfully, this passage makes it clear that real Christians (including John himself) *do* sin, but there is a remedy for it. Confession to God (that is, agreeing with him about our sin) brings God's forgiveness and cleansing! This is the powerful answer to sin in the life of believers!

So, if your goal is to see how much you can sin and not go to hell, then you are probably not a real Christian. You may attend a church, even join a church, sing in the choir, teach a Sunday school class and be on the church board, but if your goal is to sin as much as possible, you are most likely not a born-again, surrendered, redeemed, saved Christian. You need to come before the Lord, confess your desire to sin and ask him to forgive you and cleanse your heart from that desire (1 John 1:9; 1 Thessalonians 4:3-7).

GOD IS NOT MOCKED

We need to remember that God does not play games. We deceive ourselves when we think we can outsmart him or get around his commands. He has called us to surrender to his will, be full of his Spirit and pure in heart, maturing in Christ; he is not satisfied with anything less. As Paul says in Galatians 6:7, "Do not be deceived, God is not mocked; for whatever a man sows, this he will also reap." Other people only see our outward appearance and the public image we show them, but God knows the intentions of our hearts—he isn't fooled. He knows whether we are really seeking him and his holiness or just playing the church game to try to look good and keep ourselves out of hell.

So, in answer to the question of this chapter, if you want to see how much sin you can get away with and still avoid hell, you are fooling only yourself. God knows your heart and you need to respond to his deep, perfect knowledge of you and all of your desires, intentions and thoughts with true repentance, confession and faith in Jesus' death on the cross. Then God will give you a true Christian life, and you will seek to sin as little as possible from that day on. As Jesus told the woman caught in adultery, "Go. From now on sin no more" (John 8:11).

PRAYING THE PRINCIPLE

Lord, give me victory over the sins in my life. I want to live for you. I want to die to sin and live in your purity, your power and your presence. Break the chains, Lord, and release me from all my prisons!

If we confess our sins, He is faithful and righteous to forgive us our sins and to cleanse us from all unrighteousness. (1 John 1:9)

Consider yourselves to be dead to sin, but alive to God in Christ Jesus. (Romans 6:11)

DISCUSSING THE PRINCIPLE

1. What was the author's original response to the young man who asked how much a Christian could sin and still go to heaven?

2. What is James's answer to the question?

3. What is Paul's answer to the question?

4. What is John's answer to the question?

5. What does it say about someone whose goal is to see how much he or she can sin and get away with it?

6. According to Galatians 6, why is it impossible to mock God in these things?

13

What Is the Best Way
to Study the Bible?

You cannot be a mature, godly Christian without serious study of God's Word. There is no substitute for it. Everything in our Christian walk depends on it. A college friend tried an experiment. He really wanted to learn the Bible, so he put a Bible under his pillow at night and asked God to put its content into his mind. The result? He ended up with a pain in his neck! No Bible knowledge comes through osmosis—you have to study!

But how does a person study the Bible? Well, there are as many methods as there are Christians. Some are good, but some are terrible. I had a friend who ascribed to the finger-in-the-text method. He'd ask God to guide him, and then, with his eyes closed, he would open the Bible at random and put his finger down on the text. When he opened his eyes, the text his finger was on was supposed to be God's answer to his question. I once heard a preacher ridiculing this method. He said that a friend tried it, and the verse his finger hit was, "Judas went out and hanged himself." So, he tried again and the verse came up, "Go and do likewise." That was the last time he tried that method!

THE BIBLE AND THE DYNAMICS OF HUMAN LANGUAGE

The Bible is the inspired Word of God written by human beings in ordinary human language. So the best method of Bible study considers and applies the dynamics of human language. This approach is often called inductive Bible study, since it seeks what the text actually says (*induction*) instead of trying to find proofs in the text for what the interpreter already believes (*deduction*). Inductive Bible study respects both the divine inspiration and authority of Scripture and the way human language communicates.

Human beings communicate in written form by combining two elements: material and structure. Material is the specific content of the message chosen from all the possible content that could have been used. And structure is the way the author organizes the material to convey a message. So, the first step in studying a biblical passage is to notice what kind of material is being used. There are three basic possibilities: events, people or ideas. Now, all biblical passages combine all of those kinds of material, but usually one is more prominent than the others.

For example, the book of Genesis deals mainly with people. Exodus mainly presents a series of important events. Proverbs presents ideas, as does the epistle to the Romans.

THE EXAMPLE OF PSALM 1

The first psalm offers a great opportunity to see this interplay between material and structure in action:

> How blessed is the man who does not walk in the counsel of
>   the wicked,
> Nor stand in the path of sinners,
> Nor sit in the seat of scoffers!
> But his delight is in the law of the LORD,
> And in his law he meditates day and night.
> He will be like a tree *firmly* planted by streams of water,
> Which yields its fruit in its season
> And its leaf does not wither;
> And in whatever he does, he prospers.
>
> The wicked are not so,
> But they are like chaff which the wind drives away.

Therefore the wicked will not stand in the judgment,
Nor sinners in the assembly of the righteous.
For the LORD knows the way of the righteous,
But the way of the wicked will perish.

Psalm 1 combines people and ideas to convey its message, but the ideas are more prominent than the people. Now, let's look at the structure of this passage. There are six structural connections that are used most frequently in written communication:

1. *Contrast.* Two elements are presented, one of which is the opposite of the other. Some terms that indicate contrast are *but, however, on the other hand, not so.*

2. *Comparison.* Two elements are presented and their similarity is stressed. Some terms that indicate comparison are *like, compared to, similar to, in the same way.*

3. *Cause-effect.* One thing causes or produces another. Some terms that indicate cause-effect are *therefore, so, in such a way that.*

4. *Effect-cause.* The first element is the result of the second one. Some terms that indicate effect-cause are *for, because, since, given that.*

5. *Climax.* The material builds to a high (or low) point.

6. *Means-goal.* The material is organized to include the person who does something, the means he or she uses to do it, and the goal reached by doing that. Some terms that indicate means-goal are *so that, in order that, in order to.*

Those six structural connections are extremely important for careful inductive Bible study. They unlock the author's intentions and message in a way that most other methods don't. If you want to improve your Bible study, write those six structural connections on a piece of paper and put it in your Bible. Refer to it as you read and see if the verse you are studying has any of those structures in it. They will open up the message of the passage in surprising ways. Let's apply that to Psalm 1.

PSALM 1

> How blessed is the man who does not *walk* in the counsel of
> the *wicked*,
> Nor *stand* in the path of *sinners*,
> Nor *sit* in the seat of *scoffers*!

This verse is structured around *effect-cause*, even though none of the
indicating terms are present. *Blessed* is the effect; and the rest of the
verse is the cause. Now note the progression of the verbs: walk, stand
and sit. This is a negative climax in which the person goes from bad
to worse in accepting the influence of evil people. First, he walks in
their counsel; then he stands in their path; and finally he sits in their
seat. Also note that the description of the evil people gets progres-
sively worse: wicked, sinners, scoffers. This is the picture of someone
sinking deeper and deeper into the ways, the influence, of evil people.
He is blessed if he does not do this!

> *But* his delight is in the law of the LORD,
> And in His law he meditates day and night.

This verse begins with *but*. What does this indicate? A *contrast!* The
first verse tells us what the blessed man does not do. On the other
side of the equation: what does he do? His delight is in God's law, on
which he meditates day and night. So, he is not influenced by evil
people, *but* he receives input from the law of God. He meditates on
God's law because he delights in it. This psalm introduces the alternatives. It represents a basic choice in life that we must all make. Will
we be influenced by the evil people around us, or will we find guidance
in the Word of God?

> He will be *like* a tree firmly planted by streams of water,
> Which yields its fruit in its season
> And its leaf does not wither;
> And in whatever he does, he prospers.

Here we have the word *like*, which indicates a comparison. So, the one who delights in God's law and meditates on it day and night is *like* a tree. What kind of tree? He is like a tree "planted firmly by streams of water." How is a person who receives guidance from God's law like a tree that is planted by a stream? He is well-nourished! The tree in this psalm is truly remarkable: it bears fruit, but its leaves never fall. It has a tremendous amount of life in it. The blessed man who doesn't allow evil people to influence him but who saturates his life with God's law prospers in whatever he does. He is like that well-nourished, full-of-life tree!

> The wicked are *not so*,
> *But* they are *like* chaff which the wind drives away.

What an amazing verse! It contains *not so*, *but* and also *like*. So, we should expect a strong contrast with a comparison too. And that is exactly what we find: the wicked are *not like* the blessed man who is *like* a well-nourished tree, *but* they are *like* chaff that the wind drives away. Chaff is the outer husk of the grain. It is dead and lifeless, and farmers allow the chaff to be blown away by the wind to separate it from the grain. Do you see the contrast of the wicked with the blessed and how this comparison makes it clear that the wicked are not like the blessed? They have no life in them.

> *Therefore*, the wicked will not stand in the judgment,
> Nor sinners in the assembly of the righteous.

This verse begins with *therefore*, so it must be giving us the effect of some cause that went before it. Because of the contrast between the blessed man and the wicked, one being dead and the other alive and well-nourished, the effect is that the wicked won't be able to stand in judgment, and sinners won't be able to stand in the righteous people's assembly. They have no standing. They will be judged. They have no divine life in them, so they will face judgment and not be able to withstand it.

> *For* the Lord knows the way of the righteous,
> *But* the way of the wicked will perish.

This verse contains two indicating terms: *for*, which indicates effect-cause, and *but*, which indicates a structure of *contrast*. Verse 6 explains the preceding verses, telling us why those statements are true. It is because the Lord knows the righteous person's way. The word *know* means to know intimately and to be united with someone. The Lord is intimately united with the way of the righteous. *But* that is not the case for the way of the wicked, so their way will perish.

This psalm introduces all the other psalms so well because it sets up the two possibilities for human life. One pictures what we should not do: take direction from evil people. The other pictures what we should do: take direction from God through his law, delight in it, meditate on it day and night. The results are evident. The wicked person's way is dead, lifeless, worthless and separated from God, but the blessed person's way is spiritually alive, well-nourished, prosperous and united with the Lord. The psalmist has set out the two choices available to us: be led by this wicked world and perish, or be led by God's law and live. Blessed people have made the right choice, and God involves himself intimately in their lives. Wicked people have made the wrong choice and end up with no place to stand in the final judgment. They are separated from the righteous and from God.

Do you see how the structural connections open up the message of the text? It is worthwhile to learn them and use them as you study God's Word. The last stage of inductive Bible study, after identifying the dominant material and the structural connections, is to apply the message to your life. I have already done that with Psalm 1. Its message is as relevant now as it was when it was written centuries ago. We must all make that choice and then live it out in our daily walk as we ignore the world's counsel and listen to the Word of God. One example of a detailed application of the message of this psalm would sound something like this: *Lord, with your help, I will protect my mind from television programs that encourage me to think the way the world thinks. Instead, I will spend one hour per day really studying your Word.*

For further practice of this method of Bible study, see the appendix for a chance to apply them to Mark 2.[1]

Happy Bible study!

PRAYING THE PRINCIPLE

How can I ever thank you enough for your Word, Lord? It is my light, my guide, my teacher, my wisdom and my treasure. I love your Word. Help me to live it out in my life for your glory and your kingdom's sake.

I will keep Your law continually,
Forever and ever.
And I will walk at liberty,
For I seek Your precepts.
I will also speak of Your testimonies before kings
And shall not be ashamed.
I shall delight in Your commandments,
Which I love.
And I shall lift up my hands to Your commandments,
Which I love;
And I will meditate on Your statutes. (Psalm 119:44-48)

DISCUSSING THE PRINCIPLE

1. Why is serious Bible study so important for Christians? How important is it to you?

2. What is inductive Bible study?

3. What are the two basic elements of any written communication?

4. What are the six structural connections the author presents?

5. Read through Psalm 1 and be able to pick out and explain the details of the structural connections in each verse.

6. Give your own summary of the message of Psalm 1 and compose a prayer that applies that message to some specific area of your life.

14

How Do I Know
God's Will for My Life?

Rick, a Christian college student, came to me with a very curious request. "Dr. Hundley, would you please pray to God and ask him what he wants to do with my life, and then tell me?" I asked, "Why don't you just ask him yourself?" "Because I don't know whether or not I want to do it," he answered. I almost laughed! Then I responded, "God doesn't play that game, Rick." At least he was honest. Many people feel the same way but are ashamed to admit it. I shared some biblical principles with him about why we should want to do the will of God and how to know it, but he became uncomfortable, made excuses and rushed off to class. Many people have trouble discerning God's will for their lives, and there are many opinions about how to do it. As a missionary I was often asked how I knew God had called me to the "mission field" (whatever that is!). I'd have to say that when I was a very young Christian, I had the same problem, so I did a four-day Bible study on the will of God. When I finished that study I was convinced of three things: (1) God has a perfect plan for my life; (2) he wants me to seek his will without conditions or reservations; and (3) he is willing to communicate his will to me if I will seek him with my whole heart.

During my journey with the Lord over the past forty-five years, two passages have been especially significant to me in my feeble attempts to know and do God's will. They are Romans 12:1-2 and the entire book of Acts. I'd like to share them with you.

TEACHINGS FROM ROMANS 12

Therefore, I urge you, brethren, by the mercies of God, to present your bodies a living and holy sacrifice, acceptable to God, *which is your spiritual* [or rational] *service of worship*. And do not be conformed to this world, but be transformed by the renewing of your mind, so that you may *prove what the will of God is*, that which is good and acceptable and perfect. (Romans 12:1-2, emphasis added)

This passage from Paul's great epistle to the Christians in Rome is full of excellent advice about knowing the will of God. The phrase in italics reveals the purpose of these verses: to enable us to prove what God's will is. The word *prove* in Greek means "to demonstrate something through your own experience." It is one thing to believe that God has a will for our lives; it is another thing to prove what it is in our own experience. Here Paul also describes God's will as "good and acceptable and perfect." It is supremely important that we believe that God's will is good, acceptable (or well-pleasing) and perfect if we are going to seek it. Many people are afraid of God's will, so they don't seek it with their whole heart. We have to trust God well enough to believe that his will is the best, even if it isn't the easiest way to live.

My wife, Sharyn, was frightened to ever be a missionary. She had a horrible fear of bugs, snakes and animals in general, plus anxiety over leaving her family, trying to learn a new language and fitting into a new culture. When we left the United States, she cried on the plane, even though she knew she was doing God's will. But when we began our ministry in Colombia, she discovered her true niche in life and enjoyed it tremendously. When we had to leave Colombia and return home, she sobbed on the plane for over two hours. She had fallen in love with Colombia, the Colombian people and the missionary life. God knows us better than we know ourselves. We can trust him!

Living for the glory of God, to fulfill his plan for our lives, is the most satisfying, exciting life anyone could ever hope to live! If you're not convinced of that, read about God's heroes in his Word and see what God did through them. Then ask God to change your heart and help you trust him for your future. That faith in the goodness of God's will is the absolutely necessary prerequisite for knowing his will for your life.

Romans 12:1-2 outlines two clear steps for knowing God's will:

1. As a result of all that God has done for you, present your body to God, making yourself a living, holy sacrifice to him. This is the first step in knowing God's will: absolute surrender. Give yourself to him for whatever he wants you to do. The wise old preachers used to say, "Give God a blank piece of paper with your signature at the bottom and ask him to fill it in with whatever he wants you to do." Don't hold anything back. It often helps to picture the worst-case scenario of what God could call you to do and then surrender to that. This doesn't mean that God will make you do the worst thing you can imagine (as some people think!). It means that your surrender to God's will as a living sacrifice must be so complete and unreserved that it even includes that possibility. So, surrender yourself to God and his will, whatever it may be.

2. Don't be conformed to this world, but let God transform you by renewing your mind. The world we live in values four main things: money, power, pleasure and comfort. A second step to knowing God's will is deciding that these values will not dominate your life. You must value God's will for your life more than being rich, more than being comfortable, more than having status and influence, and more than your personal pleasure. Again, this is a trust issue. Does God or the world know what's best for you? Have you honestly made the decision that doing God's will is primary and everything else in your life is secondary? If not, ask God to touch your heart, transform your mind and convince you. Paul says that God can renew your mind; that is, he can give you a new way of thinking, new priorities, new goals and new values. As God renews your mind, you will find it easier and easier to seek God's will with all your heart.

THE MODEL IN THE BOOK OF ACTS

Now that we have looked at the pregame warm-up for knowing God's will, it's important to see how God's will works out practically in his Word. How do people actually find God's will in the Bible? The book of Acts gives us an excellent example. The book of Acts is an especially good source of information of how Christians lived after the resurrection, seeking God's guidance about the big decisions in their lives.

I have counted more than two hundred decisions made by Christians in Acts. Most of those decisions were based on principles from the Old Testament or from the teachings of Jesus. For example, Jesus told his disciples to flee persecution, and those early Christians had ample opportunity to put that principle into practice! And Jesus' commandments to his disciples about preaching, teaching, healing and casting out demons were put into practice by those first Christians. They also used principles from the Old Testament to guide their actions (see, for example, Acts 4:24-30; 15:12-21). But there are thirty decisions recorded in Acts that were not based solely on principles from the Old Testament or the teachings of Christ. Those thirty decisions were based on God's direct, personal guidance. These divide into three groups of ten: where God wanted them to go, what God wanted them to do and what was going to happen.

Those thirty decisions came at strategic moments in their lives when Old Testament principles and Jesus' teaching could have taken them in more than one acceptable direction. God used many means to speak to them. Sometimes God spoke through visions (Acts 10:3-5; 10:10; 16:6-10; 18:9-10). Sometimes he spoke through prophets (Acts 11:28-30; 21:10-11). Sometimes he spoke to a group of people (Acts 13:1-4; 15:28; 16:10), and sometimes to an individual (Acts 9:6, 11; 20:23; 23:11). Though the methods of guidance changed, one thing remained constant throughout—their attitude of obedience and sensitivity to his voice. They were certain that God was speaking to them and immediately did what he told them to do. It is clear that they had learned to recognize God's voice when he spoke to them, and they longed to know and do his will. As Jesus said, the good shepherd

(Jesus) "goes ahead of them, and the sheep follow him because they know his voice" (John 10:4). Knowing his voice takes practice and deep trust. We become familiar with Jesus as we increasingly spend time with him. Many people feel supernatural peace in their soul when God has spoken to them. Again, that can only come from long times of personal fellowship with the Lord as we learn to recognize his voice and feel his peace in our hearts. It does seem that God has made sure that if we want to know his will for our lives, we must draw close to him in intimate fellowship and surrender to his good will— two birds with one stone!

So, what is the pattern established in Acts for knowing God's will? Most decisions are made on the basis of biblical principles from the Old Testament or from the teachings of Jesus. But every now and then the early Christians were called upon to make a decision in which biblical principles could have been applied in more than one way. In those cases the Lord stepped in directly to show them his will. I believe that this is the Christian pattern for knowing God's will. Christians should base most decisions on the teachings of Scripture, but when Scripture could lead in more than one acceptable direction, we must trust the Lord to direct us.

It is clear that this pattern depends on a thorough knowledge of the Word of God. We need to saturate ourselves with God's Word so that our decisions flow naturally from its teachings. This does not happen by osmosis but requires disciplined, serious study of the Bible on a daily basis.

When we get to one of those important decisions in our lives, in which God's Word could take us in more than one direction, we can go boldly and confidently to the Lord in prayer, asking him to reveal his will to us directly. Many crucial decisions in our lives fall into this category: whom should I marry, what should I study, what should I do with my life, where should I live, what job should I take, how should I serve the Lord when I retire? Note that in each case there are biblical principles to narrow down the possible decisions. You wouldn't want to waste your time asking God if you should be a drug dealer or a pimp! But within the boundaries outlined in God's Word, there are many people you could marry, many courses you could study, many jobs you could take, and many places you could live. It is at those points that God is willing to step in and guide you directly if you have learned to listen to his voice and really want to do his will more than anything else. We are commanded in Scripture to "understand what the will of the Lord is" (Ephesians 5:17) and to "be filled with the knowledge of His will" (Colossians 1:9). We are all called to know God's will as it is revealed in his Word and to seek his guidance in the crossroads of life. All of this is based on the truth we saw earlier about presenting ourselves to God, not conforming to this world but being transformed by the renewing of our minds. Total surrender is the key to knowing the will of God.

I often think of that college student who asked me to seek God's will for him. He was studying to be a pastor. I hope he finally decided to seek God's will with his whole heart. I'd hate to think that he might have missed out on the joy, satisfaction and excitement of following God's will wherever it leads. His ministry and life would be richer if he did. Rick, if you're out there, please write me!

If we are going to marry the partner the Lord has for us, study the courses he wants us to learn, live where he wants us to live and serve him in the vocation he has planned for us, we must know and obey God's will. I am married to the one woman God chose for me among all the women on earth. Praise God! I am living in the place he chose for me, doing the job he has called me to do. Is there any happier, more fulfilling existence anyone can experience on this planet? I don't think so, and I treasure this same reality for every Christian I know.

PRAYING THE PRINCIPLE

Lord, I want to do your will more than I want to live. Guide me, lead me, show me what you want me to do with my life, and with your help I will do it with joyous abandon.

Therefore, I urge you, brethren, by the mercies of God, to present your bodies a living and holy sacrifice, acceptable to God, *which is* your spiritual [or rational] service of worship. And do not be conformed to this world, but be transformed by the renewing of your mind, so that you may prove [in your own experience] what the will of God is, that which is good and acceptable and perfect. (Romans 12:1-2)

DISCUSSING THE PRINCIPLE

1. What does the last part of Romans 12:2 teach about knowing God's will? Why is it so important to trust God's will as the best for your life? Do you?

2. Once we have established our trust in God and our desire to know his will, what is the first step toward knowing God's will in Romans 12? Has that happened in your life? Are you asking God to do that right now?

3. What is the second step to knowing God's will in Romans 12? How easy is that? Why?

4. Name some of the decisions made in the book of Acts that were based on the Old Testament or Jesus' teachings. Are biblical principles the main way you know God's will for your daily life? What do you have to do to make that work?

5. Based on thirty decisions in the book of Acts, what are the three areas in which God directly led the early Christians? How do they differ from decisions based on the Old Testament or the teachings of Jesus? Why are those thirty events so important for us?

6. What is the pattern for knowing and doing God's will that is established in the book of Acts? How does that apply to you?

15

Does God Always Heal
Us If We Have Enough Faith?

Marilyn and Tom were a young couple that we led to faith in Christ while we were preparing to leave for language school in Costa Rica, before going to Colombia. They became vibrant Christians, and soon afterward they felt God's call to ministry. Tom went to seminary and became a pastor. Early in his ministry Tom was diagnosed with cancer. Someone in a prayer group they attended gave a "word of prophecy" that Tom would be on his deathbed but God would raise him up. A few months later, he died. Marilyn wrote us and told us that she was about to lose her mind over all that had happened. She wrote, "It's not Tom's death; I can live through that. But right after the funeral, some people from that prayer group came to visit me and told me that if I had used more faith, Tom would still be alive. I'm afraid of losing my mind with the grief and the guilt that I feel!"

We immediately wrote Marilyn and assured her that what they said wasn't true, but she struggled with the pain of that guilt for years afterward. I can't think of many more destructive things that can happen to a person than having to live with a feeling of guilt over not having enough faith to save a loved one from death. The cruelty of that attack on Marilyn is heartbreaking and certainly not based on the Word of God.

Today, the church is being bombarded with teaching on healing that seems to say that if you have enough faith, you will always be healed. Proof texts are produced that seem to support this belief, and televangelists show case after case from all over the world in which people have been miraculously healed under their ministries. In the middle of all of this, humble Christians wonder if they have shortchanged themselves and their loved ones by not following the "name it and claim it" doctrine. Extreme prosperity theology teaches people that if they have enough faith in God, they will be healthy, wealthy and successful. This tide of erroneous teaching is sweeping over the church around the world, with devastating effects in many people's lives.

Stan was a sincere young Christian who desired to learn about living by faith. He also had epilepsy, but it was controlled by medications. One day, Stan attended a service in which the preacher told the group that God has promised to heal any disease, and if you depend on doctors and medicines, you are calling God a liar. Stan didn't want to do that, so he went home and poured all of his epilepsy meds down the drain. Two days later, he suffered a grand mal seizure that almost killed him. As a result, Stan went back on his meds, but he left the church and told me over the phone that, "Christianity is a lie. It doesn't work. I had faith, but God wouldn't help me." I tried to explain to him that what he had heard from that preacher was contrary to the Bible, but to no avail. We never saw him again.

I wish I had been able to offer him something in writing like this chapter. Let's look at this issue and see what God's Word really teaches about healing.

BIBLICAL TEACHING ON HEALING

1. God heals people, and there are people who have the gift of healing. God's Word records dozens of cases in which people were supernaturally healed by his power. Although it is a fact that God doesn't usually heal people, it is also true that many times he does. I don't know any Christians who have not at some time experienced God's healing power in their own lives or in the lives of their loved ones. I have been healed, and I have seen God heal many people as I prayed for them.

It is also clear in Scripture that some people have a unique gift of healing. Paul writes that "to each one is given the manifestation of the Spirit for the common good. . . . For to one is given . . . gifts of healing by the one Spirit" (1 Corinthians 12:7-9). Paul is an excellent example of this. In Acts 19:11-12, we read that, "God was performing extraordinary miracles by the hands of Paul, so that handkerchiefs or aprons were even carried from his body to the sick, and the diseases left them and the evil spirits went out." What an incredible testimony that is of God's great power through a man! By the way, Paul made it clear that not everyone has healing gifts: "All do not have gifts of healings, do they?" (1 Corinthians 12:30). In the body of Christ, we need each other because God has given each of us gifts. No one has all of the gifts, and there is no gift more important than any other one (see 1 Corinthians 12:4-21).

2. Some people fake the gift of healing and defraud people for money. There is an example of attempting to use healing for the wrong purposes in the book of Acts. Simon was converted to faith in Christ out of the world of sorcery. When he saw the miracles performed by the apostles through the power of the Holy Spirit, Simon offered Philip and Peter money to give him the power of the Holy Spirit. Peter answered, "May your silver perish with you, because you thought you could obtain the gift of God with money!" Peter told Simon to repent of his terrible sin, and Simon seemed to respond positively to that reprimand (Acts 8:5-24).

Still today there are those who use healing to feed their greed. There are many eyewitness accounts of "healers" using electric shock chairs to give seekers a *jolt*, employing stooges to come forward and pretend to be healed, and insisting that God always heals if you have enough faith (and give a substantial offering!). Paul calls these people "false apostles, deceitful workers" (2 Corinthians 11:11-15). He makes it clear that he and his disciples never received money from converts when they evangelized them. They never made themselves "a burden" to them (2 Corinthians 12:12-18). How different that is from some of the multimillion-dollar ministries today that promise people health, wealth and success if they will just send in "their best gift" for the ministry! I must say that I am often amazed at how many faith healers wear glasses as they preach! What happened? Couldn't God heal their sight? Sometimes these claims appear especially ludicrous, even cruel and heartless.

I was visiting in the home of a senior citizen who had been supporting a faith healer's ministry for many years. Her husband had died, so she wrote the healer's ministry to tell them that she could no longer afford to pay her pledge, but that she would be praying daily for their ministry. She showed me the letter they wrote back. In it they warned her that God had protected her as long as she was giving to the ministry and was under the protection of their prayers, but they could not say what might happen to her if she quit giving and came out from under that protective blessing. I was incensed! This kind of thing has to stop. It is cruel, heartless and shameful.

3. The Bible does not *teach that God always heals if we have enough faith*. The great apostle Paul, a man of astonishing faith and power, is an excellent example of this truth. I doubt that anyone today could claim to even come close to his faith and healing gifts. Did this great man of faith practice the "God always heals" philosophy? He did not.

Timothy, one of Paul's converts, was called to ministry in the early church. Paul charged Timothy as his "true child in the faith" to fulfill the ministry that God had given to Timothy (1 Timothy 1:2). But Timothy had a problem. According to Paul, Timothy suffered from "frequent ailments" (1 Timothy 5:23). Did Paul tell Timothy to gather his leaders, have them lay hands on him and heal him? No. His advice was, "No longer drink water *exclusively*, but use a little wine for the sake of your stomach and your frequent ailments" (1 Timothy 5:23). What happened to the "word of faith," the anointing, the laying on of hands? Paul ignored all of the things modern faith healers preach so strongly. Instead, he suggested that his son in the Lord drink a little bit of wine to heal his stomach and "frequent ailments."

Paul also shares with Timothy that one of Paul's companions, Trophimus, became ill and left him sick at Miletus (2 Timothy 4:20). If the Lord always heals, and if Paul, obviously a man of tremendous faith, had healing gifts, why did he leave this man in Miletus? The answer is simple: God does not always heal, not even for the great apostle Paul.

The most telling example of this is the life of Paul himself. Paul writes that he experienced a "thorn in the flesh" which was "a messenger of Satan to torment me—to keep me from exalting myself!" (2 Corinthians 12:7). He admitted that he had prayed three times for the Lord to remove it, but the Lord's answer was, "My grace is sufficient for you, for power is perfected in weakness" (vv. 8-9). Paul saw this as an opportunity to boast in his own weakness so that people would more easily see the power of God in his life (vv. 9-10). Of course, the million-dollar question is, "What was the thorn in Paul's flesh?" Though there have been many suggestions, we may never know what it was. Perhaps that was his intention, so that each of us could insert our own "thorn" into Paul's dialogue with God. Whatever weakness we may have, God's grace is sufficient for us because God enjoys perfecting his power in our weakness.

However, there seem to be many indicators in the New Testament that Paul's thorn may well have been disease, probably affecting his eyes. In Galatians 4:13-14, Paul reminds them, "You know that it was because of a bodily illness that I preached to you the gospel the first time; and that which was a trial to you in my bodily condition you did not despise or loathe, but you received me as an angel of God, as Christ Jesus *Himself*." But what was this "bodily illness"? In verse 15, Paul says, "I bear you witness that, if possible, you would have plucked out your eyes and given them to me." He had eye trouble, and it probably made him look awful.

Did this illness make it hard for Paul to see? It appears so. At the end of this epistle, he wrote, "See with what large letters I am writing to you with my own hand" (Galatians 6:11). Paul says something similar in 1 Corinthians 16:21 ("the greeting is in my own hand—Paul"), and in 2 Thessalonians 3:17, he writes, "I, Paul, write this greeting with my own hand, and this is a distinguishing mark in every letter; this is the way I write." Apparently, some people had been forging letters saying they were from Paul, so he made sure that they could recognize his signature. Paul had an *amanuensis* (a secretary) who actually wrote the other parts of his letters. Why? It wasn't because he was illiterate—he was well educated. But the idea that he could not see well would effectively explain the situation.

As you can see, the evidence that this "thorn" was an eye disease is not definitive. It may well have been something else. Many fine biblical scholars have assumed that Paul's thorn is described in 2 Corinthians 12:7-10. There Paul writes, "I am well content with weaknesses, with insults, with distresses, with persecutions, with difficulties, for Christ's sake; for when I am weak, I am strong" (v. 10). That is certainly possible. In chapter 11, Paul gives a list of the things he suffered in ministry (danger, hardship, hunger, thirst, etc.). He then adds, "Apart from *such* external things, there is the daily pressure on me *of* concern for all of the churches" (v. 28). Paul had a great deal of suffering in his life, and any of it could have been his "thorn." Be that as it may, Paul experienced illness (Galatians 4:13-15). He suffered from bodily illness that was not instantaneously cured. He probably had serious eye trouble. His disciples Timothy and Trophimus also suffered from illnesses that were not immediately healed. Let's face it, if the apostle Paul struggled with illness, we will too!

4. What about those passages in the New Testament that seem to promise that God will always heal us if we have enough faith? There are several key passages in the New Testament that the Word of Faith movement uses to claim that, if we have enough faith, we will always be healed (such as Matthew 8:16-17; 1 Peter 2:24). Many of them contain tremendous promises from God that we should hold onto by faith. Still, these passages must be understood within the broader context of the entire Word of God. The main passage that is preached and taught to encourage belief in automatic healing by faith is James 5:14-16.

In this passage, James, the leader of the church in Jerusalem, presents the proper steps to be taken in the local church when someone is sick. He states,

> Is anyone among you sick? *Then* he must call for the elders of the church and they are to pray over him, anointing him with oil in the name of the Lord; and the prayer offered in faith will restore the one who is sick, and the Lord will raise him up, and if he has committed sins, they will be forgiven him. Therefore, confess your sins to one another, and pray for one another so that you may be healed. The effective prayer of a righteous man can accomplish much.

Many faith healers read this passage and then pronounce, "Case closed! God always heals in response to the believing prayer of the leaders of the church!" But we need to look at that passage carefully to see exactly what it is and is not saying. It contains an incredibly powerful promise, but it is not the promise of automatic, instantaneous healing if the leaders of the church have sufficient faith.

JAMES 5 ON HEALING

There are five questions to consider in this passage:

1. What does the term sick *in verse 14 mean?* The Greek word for "sick" in this passage is *astheneō*, and its primary meaning is "weakness." It can be used for sickness, but it usually refers to the inability to do what should be done. Today, *asthenia* is used by doctors to describe physical weakness or fatigue. *Astheneō* is used in the following passages:

- In 1 Corinthians 15:43, Paul states that in death our bodies are planted in *weakness* (*astheneō*) but raised in power (*dynamis*).

- 2 Corinthians 13:4 declares that Jesus was crucified because of *weakness* (*astheneō*), but he lives by God's power (*dynamis*).

- In Romans 6:19, Paul tells his readers that he has to speak to them in human terms because of the *weakness* (*astheneō*) of their flesh.

- Romans 8:26 insists that the Spirit helps us in our *weakness* (*astheneō*) because we don't know how to pray as we should.

- Hebrews 5:2 even declares that Jesus was subject to *weakness* (*astheneō*) just as we are (see also Hebrews 4:15; 11:34).

All of these passages use the same term we find in James 5:14, and not one of them is describing physical sickness. They are all talking about *weakness* in the sense of inability to do something, or *weariness*. Now, there are other passages that use it to refer to physical illness (Luke 13:12; John 5:3; Acts 28:9; 1 Timothy 5:23; 2 Corinthians 12:9; Galatians 4:13), but it often refers to weakness, not illness. So, we can't be too dogmatic about its use in James 5. Let's look at the context of the rest of the passage to see which translation seems the most appropriate.

2. How is the word sick *used in verse 15?* The Greek word for *sick* in verse 15 is *kamnonta*, from the verb *kamnō*, and its basic meaning is *weary* or *worn out*. The only other appearance of this Greek term in the New Testament is in Hebrews 12:3, where the writer says not to "grow *weary* and lose heart." It does not imply physical sickness.

3. What about the statement in verse 15 that "the prayer offered in faith will restore *the one who is sick [weary/worn out]"?* The word *restore* is the Greek verb *sōzō*. That term is used in the Greek New Testament both for spiritual salvation and for physical deliverance or healing. The verb *sōzō* is used in eighty-six passages in the New Testament. It refers to spiritual salvation sixty-one times and to physical healing or deliverance twenty-five times. Again, this term is used much more for spiritual salvation than it is for physical healing or deliverance. It is often related to salvation from sin and forgiveness of sins. More significantly, James uses this verb five times in his epistle, and four of those five times it is obviously referring to spiritual salvation (James 1:21; 2:14; 4:12; 5:20). The only questionable use of the term is in James 5:15: Does it refer to spiritual salvation or physical healing? It would certainly be confusing on James's part to use it spiritually three times in his letter and then use it physically in verse 15, followed by another spiritual use of it five verses later in verse 20. That doesn't seem likely, does it?

4. What does the passage say about sin? A crucial question is what verse 15 says about sin. This will help us determine the overall meaning of the passage. In verse 15, James says that when the elders pray for the person, "If he has committed sins, they will be forgiven him." In verse 16, he says that believers should, "therefore, confess your sins to one another, and pray for one another so that you may be *healed*" (emphasis added). How does confession of sin bring healing? The word for "heal" in verse 16 is the Greek term *iaomai*, which usually refers to physical healing. But it can also refer to spiritual healing, that is, conversion (see Matthew 13:15; John 12:40; Acts 28:27). Confession of sin for spiritual healing or conversion is more plausible in this text than confession of sin for physical healing.

This means that James has used terms in this passage that are at best ambiguous in their meaning. The word for *sick* in verse 14 can mean either physically ill or weary (that is, unable to do something). The word for *restore* can either mean physical healing or spiritual healing (though James uses it elsewhere in his letter exclusively for spiritual salvation). The term for *healed* in verse 16 usually means physical healing, but it can also mean spiritual healing (salvation).

This passage can be read two ways: (1) that when leaders of the church pray in faith for someone who is sick and anoint the person with oil, the person will automatically be physically healed, or (2) that when elders of the church pray for people who are struggling with sin and are unable to cope with it, and anoint them with oil, if they confess their sins they will be saved, restored and renewed, and their sins will be forgiven.

Since James, his elders and his church members are all dead, I think that the second is much more likely. If this formula always worked for physical healing, wouldn't at least some of them still be alive today? And wouldn't churches where this kind of faith healing is believed and practiced be bursting at the seams with incredibly old people?

5. *What does "praying in faith" mean in this passage?* I want to think with you for a minute about the phrase "the prayer offered in faith" (v. 15). It seems to me that this phrase is crucial for understanding this text. What does it really mean to pray "in faith"? He-

brews 11, the famous faith chapter of the Bible, defines faith as "the assurance of *things* hoped for, the conviction of things not seen" (v. 1). Throughout Scripture God gives people the ability to believe him for the things that he wants to do, that they hope for and cannot yet see, and then he does them. Faith gives us the assurance that what we hope for, assuming it's God's will, is really going to happen. It provides us with conviction about things we have not yet seen. That is, it is not something we work up ourselves; it is a supernatural sight that God gives us. In 1 John 5:14-15, John explains, "This is the confidence which we have before Him, that, if we ask anything *according to His will*, He hears us. And if we know that He hears us *in* whatever we ask, we know that we have the requests which we have asked from Him" (emphasis added).

When we pray *according to God's will*, he provides what we ask for. And how do we know what his will is so that we can pray in accord with it? According to Paul, when we don't know how to pray about something, the Spirit of God "intercedes for us . . . according to *the will* of God" (Romans 8:26-27). So, when we pray for someone's healing, sometimes the Spirit gives us faith to believe that God wants to heal the person and he does just that. But that faith is not something we can muster through our own efforts or desires; it is something given to us by the Holy Spirit, who knows the will of God and helps us to pray according to God's will. That is what it means to pray "in faith," to pray "in the name of Jesus" or to pray "according to the will of God."

Bear in mind that Paul says, "To each one is given the manifestation of the Spirit for the common good. For to one is given the word of wisdom through the Spirit, and to another the word of knowledge according to the same Spirit; to another faith by the same Spirit, and to another gifts of healing by the one Spirit" (1 Corinthians 12:7-9). So, both faith and healing are gifts of the Holy Spirit. They do not come from us. At times, the Spirit gives us faith to believe that God wants to heal someone, so we pray for the person, and God heals him or her. It is an amazing experience!

A CASE OF REAL HEALING

One night in Colombia, I received a phone call from the United States. My mother told me that my father had been infected with a brain virus. She said his fever had stayed at 105 degrees for several days and he didn't have long to live. I promised I would do everything I could to get home immediately. Through a miraculous chain of events, I was on a plane for Miami the next morning. As I flew toward the United States, I asked the Lord to give me a sermon for my dad's funeral. I turned page after page in my Bible, asking the Lord to show me what he wanted me to preach at the funeral service. I couldn't find anything. All of a sudden the Lord spoke to my heart and assured me that my dad was not going to die. He would recover from this illness. I was thrilled! When I arrived in Miami, my relatives took me straight to the hospital room where my dad's life was rapidly ebbing away. As I donned protective clothing, my father's doctor told me that there was no hope—Dad was going to die. And even if he were to live by some miracle, he would be a vegetable the rest of his life—his brain was cooked. I responded, "I know that God is going to heal my dad and restore him." He rolled his eyes and gave me that "you poor, foolish man" look and left the room.

When I entered Dad's room, I saw all the tubes and wires connected to his body. It looked awful. I saw the electronic thermometer that was registering his temperature at 105 degrees. I placed my hand on his head and said, "Lord, I know you want to heal my dad, so please do it right now. In Jesus' name. Amen." Immediately, my brother shouted, "Look at the thermometer—it's going down!" We all stared at that needle as it descended from 105 degrees and soon registered 98.6. The next day my dad woke up and began talking to us. The following day he got out of bed on his own. Soon he was making his nurses a nervous wreck by leaving his room and walking all over the hospital! Mom jokingly said to me one day, "Did you have to pray so hard for him? He's driving us all crazy!"

Dad completely recovered and lived for many more years. In fact, he had better health after the incident than he did before it happened. That is what I believe James, Paul and John meant when they talked about praying in faith according to the will of God. I have seen God do this many times, but I have also prayed many times and not seen any healing. Though this is not an automatic process, it is glorious when God chooses to heal and enables us to pray in real faith according to his will!

The Bible makes it clear that the sick person has to have faith to be healed. Time and again, Jesus said to people, "Your faith has made you whole." This is a basic principle of God's Word. We must believe that God wants to heal us in order to be healed. Again, 1 Corinthians 12:9 says that faith is a gift given by the Holy Spirit. It is not something we work up in ourselves. It comes from God, and God responds to it miraculously. We must learn to live close enough to God so we can sense what his will is and sense his faith in us to do something miraculous. God is more than willing to work miracles in and through our lives, but it has to be on his terms, not ours. Peter makes this point clearly when he writes,

> As each one has received a *special* gift, employ it in serving one another as good stewards of the manifold grace of God. Whoever speaks, *is to do so* as one who is speaking the utterances of God; whoever serves *is to do so* as one who is serving by the strength which God supplies; *so that in all things God may be glorified through Jesus Christ, to whom belongs the glory and dominion forever and ever. Amen.* (1 Peter 4:10-11, emphasis added)

Healing ministry, like all other ministries of service, is meant to bring glory to God, not to the "healer." We are to heal "by the strength which God supplies." God longs to use our lives to do amazing things, but, as someone has said, "The world has not yet seen what God will do through someone who will give Him all the glory." So, let's glorify God as he gives us faith to do miraculous things in his name—he deserves all the honor and all the glory!

PRAYING THE PRINCIPLE

Lord, I praise you that you sometimes heal us miraculously of our diseases and sicknesses, and thus glorify your great power. But I also praise you for the times you decide not to heal us, but give us the strength to go through our sufferings in such a way that we bring glory to your name. Either way, Lord, I trust you—whether I walk on the "Praise the Lord" path or the "Praise the Lord anyway" path. Send me whatever brings you glory and I will trust you to help me in it and give me your victory through it.

> Jesus was going throughout all Galilee, teaching in their synagogues and proclaiming the gospel of the kingdom, and healing every kind of disease and every kind of sickness among the people. (Matthew 4:23)

DISCUSSING THE PRINCIPLE

1. Describe the modern problem of those who fake healing to take people's money? Have you seen this? If so, describe it.

2. What are the three biblical indicators that Paul did not practice the "God always heals" philosophy? Is there some other possible explanation for Paul's "thorn in the flesh"? What is your conclusion about Paul and sickness?

3. What does the word *sick* most likely mean in James 5:14-15?

4. What are the two possible interpretations of the meaning of James 5:14-15? Which do you think is more likely to be correct? Why?

5. What does "praying in faith" mean in this passage?

6. What is your personal conclusion about healing after reading this chapter?

PART FOUR

Questions About Other Religions

We live in an age in which the primary religious virtue is tolerance and the primary religious vice is intolerance. We are bombarded from every side by the message of multiculturalism and religious relativism. High school teachers, college professors, media stars, movies and books hammer home the argument that tolerance of others' opinions is an absolute virtue (even while they stress that there are no absolutes!). In the midst of all of this adoration of relativism and opposition to any system that claims ultimate truth, Christians are often seen to be totally out of touch with reality, living in the past and wallowing in ignorance and arrogance. It seems to be a no-win situation. But in that context we are called by our Lord to be light in a dark world, openly confessing our belief that Jesus is still "the way, the truth and the life" and that no one comes to the heavenly Father except through him. Talk about being out of step with the spirit of the age! Nevertheless, we are called by God to proclaim that truth to our generation, whether they approve or not.

How can we witness in such an environment? First, we need to be absolutely clear about what we believe and why we believe it. If God's

Word is true (and we believe it is!), it must have the last word on every issue dealing with human life. It is not debatable but is God's eternal Word—his opinion on what humans should believe and should do and not do.

So, our confidence is not in ourselves and our opinions; we must do our best to align our views with the views of God! In the cultural debate of our time, we do not pretend to be smarter or wiser or better than anyone else; our claim is that God is smarter, wiser and better than any human. In part four we will consider (1) the truthfulness of Christianity over against other religions, (2) how to respond to atheists, (3) whether Islam is a violent religion, (4) the eternal destiny of those who have never heard the gospel and (5) the uniqueness of Jesus. After considering those touchy issues, we should be better prepared to witness with humble confidence to those around us who need to hear the good news of Jesus.

16

How Do We Know
Christianity Is True and Other
Religions Are False?

I don't think I have ever finished a world religions course without having a student ask how we know Christianity is true and other religions are false. It is a reflection of the popular values of complete tolerance and personal humility. In the present climate of openness, acceptance and multiculturalism, it is shocking to hear that Christianity claims to be true and all other religions are false. This goes against the grain of Western society's sensibilities and values. As a student once put it, "Christians are so arrogant. They think they are the only ones who are right and everybody else is wrong!" It is difficult to claim the finality of Christ and the uniqueness of Christianity without appearing to be arrogant and deluded to unbelievers. However, while our position may be unpopular, it is not untenable.

NOT EVERYTHING IN OTHER RELIGIONS IS FALSE

It is important to make it clear that Christians do not believe that everything in other religions is false. In my ten years of teaching comparative religions, I have come to deeply appreciate many aspects of other religions: the dedication and commitment of Islam, the selflessness and desire to hurt no living thing in Buddhism, the moral responsibility and discipline of Hinduism. To be frank, many world religions include the Golden Rule—*Do to others as you would have them do to you*—as part of their teachings. The beauty and clarity in many religions show the epitome of human beings' ability to create lofty and ennobling thoughts. My students did not find out, until our last class together, that I am an evangelical Christian. They often expressed their amazement because I had presented other religions so fairly and sympathetically. That should not be a surprise, but Christians are often stereotyped as being smug, ignorant or dismissive of other religions. It is crucial that people understand that we do *not* reject everything in other religions and that we respect everyone's right to believe whatever he or she wants, or to not believe in anything.

SUPERNATURAL POWER IN NON-CHRISTIAN RELIGIONS

On the other hand, it is also important to explain carefully what we believe about other religions. According to Scripture, there are only two sources of supernatural power in the universe: God and Satan. So, when a religion displays supernatural power but denies the teaching of God's Word, we assume that power comes from Satan. Paul supported this idea when he stated that "the things which the Gentiles sacrifice, they sacrifice to demons and not to God" (1 Corinthians 10:20). According to Paul, demons are behind the gods worshiped by non-Christians. This is one of the major reasons Christians reject other religions as false.

I was once confronted with this situation on a flight from Medellin to Bogotá. A man and his wife sat down next to me. He was an American, she a Colombian. He asked me what I did for a living, and I responded that I was a seminary professor. He lit up and smiled as he suggested that I invite his wife to speak to the students in our seminary. I soon learned that she was "Regina Eleven"—an influential woman with supernatural powers I had previously heard of. She chimed in that she would love to speak to my students to "help them release all of their powers in God." I said I didn't think so, and she became very agitated. "You don't believe I have power? I'll show you!" She began to focus on a coke bottle in the plane's galley and it began to shake. I responded, "Please don't do that. It will just make a mess. I know you have power, but I don't believe your power is from God." I asked what she believed about heaven and hell. Regina assured me that there is no hell and that everyone goes to heaven when they die. According to God's Word, I said, that is not true. Her husband warned me, "Be careful, mister, she can do you a lot of harm." I answered, "Greater is the One who is in me than the one who is in her." That was more than she could take. She concentrated all of her powers on me. She actually began to shake, turn red in the face, and she couldn't speak. Suffice it to say, she could not do anything to me, and her husband finally had to take her to the back of the plane away from me to calm her down. That experience crystallized for me the idea of two opposing supernatural powers, with God's power being superior to Satan's, and that those who have supernatural power but reject God's Word have satanic power, even if they don't know it.

MANMADE RELIGIONS VERSUS GOD-REVEALED RELIGION

The other major epiphany that has helped me understand other religions came when I was reading the Muslim Qur'an and the Hindu Bhagavad Gita and Rig Veda in preparation for my lectures in the world religions courses. As I began to think through the differences and similarities between world religions, all of a sudden it came to me that the main difference between God-revealed religions and human religions lies in their method for obtaining salvation. Basically, religions constructed by humans rely on self-effort to obtain salvation, but God-revealed religions rely on God's grace for salvation. Humans make systems that exalt humans and their ability to save themselves through their own efforts. God makes systems that exalt him, his grace, his power and his personal love relationship with us. Look at the religious systems made by humans. Islam teaches that we can be saved by practicing the five pillars: confession, prayer, charity, fasting and pilgrimage to Mecca. People who practice these things in obedience to Allah will make it to Paradise. Hinduism is a self-atoning religion that teaches yoga practice and "willed introversion." Hindus practice meditation and focus that enables a person to see the world as it really is. Hinduism holds out the carrot of reaching *moksha* (spiritual liberation from the physical), which is achieved through personal effort and usually requires hundreds or even thousands of deaths and reincarnations to finally achieve it. Buddhism basically teaches the same thing as Hindus, but insists a person can achieve it in one lifetime if he or she tries hard enough. Buddhism also teaches that there is no god who can help a person get there; the person's own effort wins the day. Confucianism, Shintoism, Jainism, shamanism, African tribal religions, New Age religions and Native American religions follow the same pattern, teaching proper conduct and personal effort for spiritual fulfillment and salvation.

To my knowledge, there are only two religions that are not based on human effort: biblical Judaism and biblical Christianity. I stress "biblical" because both Jews and Christians have the tendency to slip into good works and human efforts to reach God, contrary to their biblical presentations. Both religions, in their biblical presentation, teach that salvation is based on the unmerited favor—grace—of God and putting faith in what he has done for his people and the whole world. In Judaism the prophets continually call the people away from empty, performance-based religion to a vital, true relationship with God. For example, in Isaiah 29:13 the prophet brings God's warning that the people

> draw near with their words
> And honor Me with their lip service,
> But they remove their hearts far from Me.

In the New Testament, Paul reminds the Ephesians that "by grace you have been saved through faith; and that not of yourselves, *it is* the gift of God; not as a result of works, so that no one may boast" (Ephesians 2:8-9). Paul's epistles to the Romans and Galatians insist that Christianity is based on salvation through faith, not works or human effort. We are not saved by good works, but we are saved to do good works (Ephesians 2:10).

Humans, it seems, naturally develop religions based on our own abilities and efforts. But God reveals that a relationship with him is based on faith in him and his grace to do for us what we can't do for ourselves. One system promotes human pride and self-sufficiency; the other requires humility, confession and self-surrender. The method of salvation quickly differentiates true religion revealed by God and religions developed by human beings.

THE UNIQUENESS OF CHRIST MAKES CHRISTIANITY UNIQUE

Finally, I believe in the unique truthfulness of Christianity because it is the only religion in which the founder lived the life he proposed, died, was buried and then was resurrected to new life. He now lives in each of his followers, giving them power and motivation to live the life he designed for them. As one student asked, "Don't you think that Buddha taught some wonderful things?" I answered, "Yes, I do. But the Buddha is no longer around to help us live out those teachings; Jesus is." That reality is what sets Christianity apart from every other religion in the world. It is not just a set of doctrines or teachings or practices to be carried out. It is a personal relationship with Jesus Christ that transforms life and prepares us for eternity. That is the unique ingredient: Jesus Christ has given his life for us and offers us a vital relationship of love and acceptance and forgiveness by him. Nothing on earth can compare. There is no competition: he is the only Savior who has given his life for humanity and is willing to live in us to help us live the "abundant life" now and usher us into eternity with him after we die. This is why Scripture records Jesus saying, "I am the way, and the truth, and the life; no one comes to the Father but through Me" (John 14:6). And this is why Peter says of Jesus Christ, "There is salvation in no one else; for there is no other name under heaven that has been given among men by which we must be saved" (Acts 4:12). Ultimately, this is why we believe that Christianity is true and all other religions are false; not because we are arrogant or prideful or deluded but because we have been totally overwhelmed by his love, his forgiveness, his grace, his power and his presence in our lives. We know of nothing else that can measure up to it. I have seen this reality played out in many people's lives.

Debbie, a Wicca student in one of my religion classes, constantly challenged Christianity and criticized what she considered to be its many faults. The last day of class, as I shared my personal testimony of conversion, she asked, "Why do you choose Jesus over all the other great religious leaders?" I shared that I had never found anyone who could compare with him. He is so loving and accepting, yet he takes sin seriously. And Jesus is still alive to transform us and free us from the power of sin in our lives. I concluded, "He is just what I need, and he has done everything he promised to do in my life."

The first day of the next semester Debbie came bounding into my classroom with an explosive smile on her face. "I did it!" she said. "I went to a church and asked Jesus into my life! And he came in! And I've never been so happy and clean and at peace in my life!" She had found the only one who can make that happen—Jesus Christ.

PRAYING THE PRINCIPLE

Lord, I thank you for revealing the path to salvation to us—the path that was opened up by Jesus' death and atonement for our sins. No manmade religion offers real salvation. They all encourage people to try to reach you on their own. Satan doesn't want anyone to come to you in faith and find forgiveness and new life. He wants everyone to believe that they can somehow make it on their own if they keep trying—and failing. Help me to communicate your gospel to others so that they can see your wonderful plan and rejoice in it. Whether they are Muslims, Hindus, Buddhists or believers in Native American spirituality, they need Jesus! He is the only one who saves. Help me to live daily like I really believe in you and act accordingly.

Being found in appearance as a man, [Jesus] humbled Himself by becoming obedient to the point of death, even death on a cross. For this reason also, God highly exalted Him, and bestowed on Him the name which is above every name, so that at the name of Jesus EVERY KNEE WILL BOW, of those who are in heaven and on earth and under the earth, and that every tongue will confess that Jesus Christ is Lord, to the glory of God the Father. (Philippians 2:8-11)

DISCUSSING THE PRINCIPLE

1. What are some of the admirable traits and teachings of non-Christian religions?

2. What is the source of supernatural power in religions that deny God's Word?

3. What is the basic difference between manmade religions and God-revealed religions? How does that play out in Islam, Hinduism and Buddhism?

4. Why are biblical Judaism and Christianity different from other religions? What does that say about how people create religions and how God reveals the truth?

5. What is the unique characteristic of Jesus that sets him apart from all other religious leaders? How was that evidenced in the life of the author's Wicca student?

6. What is your opinion about the truth of Christianity over against all other religions?

17

What Would You Say
to an Atheist?

It was the last night of our distance learning course on world religions, and I was allowing the students to ask me any questions they had, promising I would answer them according to my own personal beliefs. After the usual questions about the religions we had studied, John, a young man in the back row, raised his hand and asked, "What would you say to an atheist?" I responded that I would probably say, "You have a lot more faith than I do!" I went on to explain that anyone who can look at the universe with its beauty, complexity, interdependence and awesomeness, and conclude that it just popped into existence for no apparent reason without a Creator has a great deal more faith than I do! I find that position to be untenable and naive.

ATHEISTS AND AGNOSTICS

Over the years I have talked to many people who claimed they were atheists. When I have defined an atheist as someone who believes that God does not exist, most of them have recanted that position and claimed that they were agnostic—someone who does not know whether God exists. After making that point I always ask them what experience they've had with religion. The vast majority were raised in religious homes and then rejected that faith because of problems they saw in it. I then ask what they think God is like, if he exists.

They have supplied some pretty incredible answers, and I've had the opportunity to say, "Well, if that's what God is like, I wouldn't believe in him either." This usually shocks them a little bit, and we get to talk about false views of God that hinder people from encountering the real God.

Recently, someone close to me has left the Christian faith and proclaimed herself to be an atheist. After the initial shock and sadness, I was able to see that perhaps this is a good thing for her. The first step toward a vital relationship with God is to jettison all the false gods that stand in the way.

FALSE GODS MUST DIE!

In 1966, Professor Thomas J. J. Altizer of Emory University published a book titled *The Gospel of Christian Atheism*. That work, and similar books written by other theologians in the 1960s, set in motion the "God is dead" movement that swept through the United States during that decade. Although Altizer was probably misunderstood, his statement that God is dead lit a fire of protest and controversy among evangelical Christians. I do not agree with Altizer's position, but I agree that sometimes people's *false* concepts of God have to die before they can encounter the true God. The following are some false gods that I believe have to go:

1. The Mom-and-Dad god. Many people worship god—the Mom-and-Dad god—for no apparent reason except that their family has always done so. A faith based on the beliefs of others is not a genuine faith. As an old preacher I once heard said, "God has no grand-children!" We must challenge our family's faith and fight our way to our own, or eventually we will find that inherited faith becomes empty and meaningless.

2. The push-button god. The god of instant gratification and easy answers is the push-button god. We have a need, so we tell god about it and he meets it—pure, simple and wonderful. But what happens when he doesn't? The push-button god doesn't always come through, and if our faith is based on the idea that god will always do what we want, we will soon give up in discouragement and disappointment, and blame God for it.

3. The god of emotion. The god of emotion is experienced as a good feeling, an exultant emotion or a moment of ecstasy. Some churches whip up this kind of emotion, believing that if we haven't been swept away in an emotional frenzy, we have not really experienced worship. Needless to say, people cannot maintain this level of emotional high all the time, so this view of god sooner or later leaves them disillusioned and convinced that they don't have enough faith to be Christians. Their emotions can't keep up with their beliefs.

4. The Santa Claus god. The Santa Claus god evokes memories of sitting on the knee of the "jolly old soul" and asking him to bring us presents for Christmas because we've been very good. Many people approach God this way. They firmly believe that if they behave themselves, if they are good, God will reward them with everything they ask. A feeling of letdown inevitably ensues, just like that Christmas morning when you came downstairs and there was no red wagon under the tree. Many people go through life believing that if they "do their best and live a good life," God will reward them with heaven when they die. The Bible teaches that we can never do enough good things to merit heaven (see Isaiah 64:6; Ephesians 2:8-9). Even if we are "good for goodness' sake," the Santa Claus god will not come through for us. He is a false god.

5. The safety-net god. The safety-net god is something like a good luck charm or talisman that we pull out when we are in trouble. In everyday life, this god is forgotten, but as soon as something difficult or dangerous occurs, out he comes. "Lord, protect me; help me; save me; heal me; make everything right again!" How many soldiers have encountered this god only to lose faith in him when the bullets quit flying? The phrase that most often escapes from people's mouths in a crisis is "My God!" In many cases, there is very little content to that exclamation, just a feeling of utter desperation or shock, and the need to express it somehow. We can't have a personal relationship with the good luck charm god. He is not the true God.

6. *The fire insurance god.* Some people's concept of a god has one central element: escaping the fires of hell. They don't love their god or obey him or seek him; they just file him away in their spiritual file cabinet, ready to pull him out like an insurance policy. Right before they die, so that they can avoid hell and make it to heaven (by the "skin of their teeth"), they pull out their fire insurance policy and hope they'll make it in. This god is not part of their daily life. He's held in reserve "just in case." If we live our entire life without having fellowship with God, we shouldn't be surprised when he honors our decision for all eternity.

7. *The head-in-the-sand god.* Many people have a concept of God based on the proverbial action of the ostrich: put your head in the sand and nothing can bother you. They have no idea why they believe in God. They do not know why they believe the Bible is the inspired Word of God. They don't know why they don't believe in some other religion. And they have never really seen God do anything that couldn't be explained away by natural causes. They just believe because they believe—no evidence, no reasons, no understanding—just blind faith in faith. When challenged, they often respond, "Well, I've just always believed this way. I don't know why." This kind of faith does not stand up well in the face of conflict, adversity or attack.

8. *The prudish god.* The false god many believe in is kind of a heavenly prude, looking down on humanity and blushing over our sexual capers. Many young people reject Christianity because they have been told that sex is nasty, and from their own experience they know that's not true. In this prudish view, god is against sexuality because it is so carnal and sinful. Those who hold this view don't take into account that God created sexuality—it was his plan and he delights in it when it is enjoyed within the public, solemn commitment of marriage. If that doesn't compute for you, just read the Song of Solomon and ask yourself why it is in the Bible. It exalts sexual love in marriage, and, in some parts, it gets downright racy! God created sex and is neither afraid of it nor embarrassed by it. God joyously blesses sexual intimacy in marriage. He is no prude.

These false gods must die! I am tempted to begin a "False gods are dead!" movement to let people know that they don't have to reject the real God to free themselves from these false gods. If atheists once believed in one of these false gods but don't believe in them anymore, I am *thrilled!* They have taken the first step toward a life-changing encounter with the true God, who waits for them with loving, open arms. Clearing away the debris of these warped concepts of God opens the way to consider the possibility that God exists and wants to have a personal relationship with each of us.

THE LIMITS OF ATHEISM

Getting back to John, the student who began this inquiry, I pushed the issue, examining the implications of not believing there is a God. First, none of us knows enough to eliminate the possibility that God exists. Second, the universe gives ample evidence of an intelligent designer who planned it and put it all together. The idea that this incredible, wonderful universe just popped into existence for no apparent reason and without any intelligence behind it takes a great deal of faith! Third, if it is possible that God exists and that he has created us as communicative beings, it is logical to assume that maybe he did that so that we could communicate with each other and with him. As the class ended that night, John waited until all the other students left the classroom, then he came up to me and said, "Dr. Hundley, I want you to know that when I started this course, I was an atheist, but now I'm just an agnostic." I told him he was moving in the right direction and to keep seeking.

A CHALLENGE TO ATHEISTS

Let's face it, if the God of the universe is waiting to invade your life and relate to you on a personal level, it would be tragic to miss that awesome experience! If we reach out to him, he will come to us and reveal himself to us so clearly that we will never doubt his existence again. But that transaction requires a little faith—stepping out without all the facts—to find something beneath our feet that we couldn't see before we took that step. As his Word puts it, "Without faith it is impossible to please *Him*, for he who comes to God must believe that He is and *that* He is a rewarder of those who seek Him" (Hebrews 11:6). If you have never done it, I challenge you right now to say out loud, "God, please show yourself to me."

I made that challenge to an engineering university student in Georgia one night. Paul came with all the usual questions about God, and we talked for quite a while. I could see that he was sincere in his search for God, so I challenged him, "Paul, go someplace right now by yourself and say out loud, 'Jesus, please come into my life, forgive my sins and make me your child,' then come back and tell me what happened." Several minutes later, Paul returned with tears streaming down his cheeks and a huge smile lighting up his face. When I asked him what had happened, he answered, "He did it! He came in! I was trying to add a principle to my life, but I needed to invite a *person!* I have never felt so clean in my life!"

Paul's experience has been repeated millions of times around the world. People have turned away from their false gods. They have sought the true God with their whole heart, and he has met with them. And that divine-human encounter has transformed them and set them on the road to that total transformation of life that only Christ can give. If you have never taken that challenge, I invite you to take it right now. Find a quiet place and talk out loud to God. He will answer you. He will allow himself to be found by you, and your life will never be the same!

PRAYING THE PRINCIPLE

Lord, so many of us have been fooled into believing that you don't exist. We have been fooled into believing in gods that always fail, always disappoint, always disillusion. Lord, rid my mind of the false gods I have trusted in the past and help me today to know you, the true God, in all your splendor and glory.

The fool has said in his heart, "There is no God." (Psalm 14:1)

DISCUSSING THE PRINCIPLE

1. What is the author's answer to the title question, What would you say to an atheist? Why did he say that?

2. What is the difference between an atheist and an agnostic?

3. Why is it so important to ask unbelievers what experience they've had with religion?

4. Summarize the points made about each of the eight false gods. Share your own experience with those views of God.

5. Why must those false gods die in order to make way for true faith?

6. What three implications of atheism did the author share with his student? What was the result? Do you know anyone you should share those ideas with? Will you?

18

Is Islam a Violent Religion?

I have never taught on Islam without having a student ask if Islam is a violent religion. Most people began thinking about this issue in light of the events of September 11, 2001. That attack on American soil radically changed many Americans' concept of the Islamic faith. Nineteen Islamist terrorists hijacked four jet airliners and flew them into their targets. Two slammed into the Twin Towers of the World Trade Center, one exploded into the Pentagon, and the fourth was diverted from its intended target by the passengers onboard; the plane crashed killing all of them. In all, almost three thousand people lost their lives in those four attacks. From that time on, Islam has become associated with vicious terrorism and horrendous violence in the minds of many people.

THE FINAL INSTRUCTIONS FOR 2001

One of the factors that has led to the association of Islam and violence is the discovery of the final instructions under which those attacks were carried out. Found in the luggage of Mohamed Atta, one of the terrorists, and later in the baggage of others, this document described in great detail the relation between those terrorist attacks and the Muslim faith.

In the final instructions, the terrorists are counseled to carry out a series of spiritual actions in preparation for their mission. They are encouraged to confess all sin to God, ask him to help them to glorify him in their attacks, read the war suras (chapters) of the Qur'an, meditate on God's promises to martyrs, ask God in prayer to give them victory, read verses from the Qur'an into their hands and rub them on all their belongings (including their weapons), ask God to block the vision of their enemies, pray before and during the mission so that God will give them success and victory, remember that the women of paradise will welcome them to the pleasant gardens of paradise, and end their lives while praying as they hit their target or make their last words be, "There is no God but Allah. Muhammad is His messenger."[1]

No wonder so many people see Islam as a violent religion. These final instructions to the 9/11 terrorists are supposedly inspired by the Qur'an and guided by Allah. It is obvious that both the terrorists and the document writers were absolutely convinced that their actions were a natural outgrowth of their faith and were sanctioned by it. But were they right? Does Islam, and specifically the Qur'an, encourage violent acts of this nature, or did those terrorists and their leaders contradict the very teaching they claim to be obeying?

ISLAM AND VIOLENCE

There are several issues that must be addressed to answer this question. First, is it true that Islam was founded by Muhammad using violence? Second, what is the Muslim doctrine of jihad and how does it relate to Muslim violence? Third, do most Muslims practice their faith peacefully or violently? Let's look at each of those issues.

1. Is it true that Islam was founded by Muhammad using violence?
Yes, it is true that Islam began within a context of violence led by its founder, Muhammad. Islam began in the city of Mecca, where Muhammad was born. There, Muhammad started to preach his message of submission to Allah, which was based on the visions he said he received in a cave outside of the city. He was rejected by many for attacking the polytheism (belief in many gods) of Mecca and its famous religious shrine, the Ka'bah. But by and large the opposition to his message was peaceful, not violent, at least at the beginning. However,

when Muhammad left Mecca and became the ruler of the city of Medina, things changed radically. The leaders of Mecca, seeing his success in Medina and the army of warriors Muhammad was training, concluded that Muhammad must be preparing to attack Mecca. So they attacked first. The war went on for many years, but finally Muhammad and his warriors were victorious, and he entered Mecca as its conqueror. But Muhammad did not follow the customary pattern of killing the leaders of a city that had attacked him; he forgave them and released them if they would promise not to fight against him anymore.

So, out of necessity, yes, Islam began as a violent religion. Its warriors trained to fight to defend their faith and the prophet Muhammad. If they had not fought, Islam would have been annihilated before it had a chance to develop. That practice has characterized Islam since its beginnings. No one is allowed to attack the faith, the Qur'an or the prophet without suffering the wrath of Muslim warriors. That position is spelled out quite clearly in the Qur'an.

2. *What is the Muslim doctrine of jihad?* The doctrine of jihad forms the foundation of Islamic views on the use of violence. Al-Hajj Talib 'Abdur-Rashid, imam of the Mosque of Islamic Brotherhood in Harlem, says that *jihad* comes from the word *jahada*, which means "to struggle." He identifies three levels of jihad taught in the Hadith (an authoritative collection of sayings of the prophet Muhammad outside of the Qur'an): personal jihad, verbal jihad and physical jihad. He identifies personal jihad as "the struggle to cleanse one's spirit of sin." Verbal jihad is "the speaking of truth in the face of a tyrant." And the physical jihad is "fighting against those who fight against us."[2]

The Qur'an itself presents two different manifestations of jihad. One, referred to as the Greater Jihad, describes an internal, personal struggle within each believer to bring life fully into alignment with the will of Allah. The focus of that jihad is the month of Ramadan, during which Muslims fast during daylight hours, pray and meditate on their lives and their faith. They sincerely attempt to wage spiritual warfare against their own sins and anything in their lives that deviates from the will of Allah as expressed in the Qur'an.

The second manifestation of jihad in the Qur'an applies the same basic principle outwardly to people who are not submitted to the will of Allah and his Holy Qur'an. Called the Lesser Jihad, this doctrine teaches that every Muslim must join a "holy war" against proven enemies of Islam when it is declared by recognized Muslim authority. If a high Muslim authority issues a fatwa, or ruling, identifying some group or nation as an enemy of the faith, the Qur'an or the prophet Muhammad, it is the duty of all Muslims to unite against those persons and kill them. In the Qur'an, Muslims are commanded to annihilate anyone who attacks Islam (sura 8:12-16, 36-40; 9:1-5, 12-16, 123). These verses command Muslims to decapitate, make war against, slay and chastise unbelievers who attack their faith.

This doctrine has been put into practice many times in the history of Islam. Some Muslims mistakenly applied it to anyone who would not willingly accept Islam. There are many cases in the history of Islam in which the faith was spread at the point of a sword, with conquered people either accepting Islam or being killed as infidels. However, that application of the teachings of the Qur'an is not correct. Muhammad taught in the Qur'an that unbelievers who do not attack Islam should be tolerated and left in peace (8:59-64; 9:1-12). This injunction has not always been obeyed by Muslims, but it is the plain teaching of the Qur'an. Muhammad especially emphasized fair treatment of Jews and Christians as "people of the Book" (that is, the Old and New Testaments, on which much of the Qur'an is based).

The 9/11 attacks were clearly based on Osama bin Laden's application of jihad to America. In his speech a month after the 9/11 attacks, bin Laden stated, "God has blessed a group of vanguard Muslims, the forefront of Islam, to destroy America. . . . I tell them that these events have divided the world into two camps, the camp of the faithful and the camp of the infidels. . . . Every Muslim must rise to defend his religion."[3] Even though bin Laden was no cleric and had no authority to issue a fatwa against America, there were many Muslim clerics who supported him and agreed that the conditions for jihad had been met. They feel that America has attacked Islam by (1) placing infidel American troops in Saudi Arabia, near the Muslim holy city of Mecca; (2) supporting Israel against the Muslim Palestinians and surrounding Muslim nations; (3) attacking Muslim nations such as Afghanistan and Iraq; and (4) infiltrating Muslim societies with American pornography, music, videos, greed and secularism. For a small group of Muslim leaders, that list is more than sufficient to declare a holy war against America and to do all they can to destroy us. This radical segment of Islam is growing every day as more and more discontented, underprivileged Muslim youth are taught to blame America for their woes and give their lives to destroy us.

3. *Do most Muslims practice their faith peacefully or violently?* Fortunately, the vast majority of Muslims practice their faith peacefully and in harmony with those who are not Muslim. They have latched on to Muhammad's teaching about peaceful coexistence with those who do not actually attack Islam, and they live their faith in peacefulness and gentleness. However, there is a growing minority in Islam that is committed to violent jihad against the West in general, and especially against the United States. They represent a small percentage of Muslims, but they are very vocal, active and visible. They have the goal of establishing a world dominated by Islam, and they believe that violence and terrorism are the best weapons to use to make that happen.

MODERATE MUSLIMS

Many Muslim leaders have repudiated terrorist groups who have hijacked Islam for their own purposes and contradicted the plain teachings of the Qur'an, which speaks against killing innocents and committing suicide. Most moderate Muslims see the terrorists' actions as a denial of Islamic faith. They protest the terrorists' erroneous use of Islam to support violence and destruction, but they also understand the issues and the anguish that motivate the terrorists.

Most Muslims are *not* terrorists. Most Muslims are *not* committed to the destruction of the West. Most Muslims are *not* joining in the holy war against the West. Most Muslims are peace-loving people who want nothing to do with terrorism. They just want a decent life for themselves and their children.

So, what can we conclude? Is Islam a violent religion? As often is the case, the answer is yes and no. Yes, Islam began as a violent religion of warriors protecting their faith and their leader against vicious attacks. Yes, Muslims have sometimes forced conversion on people at the point of a sword. Yes, there is a growing segment of Islam dedicated to violence, terrorism and the destruction of the West. Yes, if Muslims see Islam being attacked and a holy war is declared by clerical authorities, Muslims are required to fight and kill the enemies of Islam.

On the other hand, no, Islam is not violent. Islam, as practiced by the vast majority of Muslims, is *not* a violent religion. It is a peaceful religion dedicated to inner purity and outer harmony.

CHRISTIANITY AND VIOLENCE

It is important to remember that Christianity also has some violent chapters in its history. The Inquisition and the Crusades were dark periods in the history of the church. And the bombing of the federal building in Oklahoma City by Timothy McVeigh, who claimed to be a Christian, is a recent example of the fact that there are bin Ladens in Christianity as well. All religions should be judged on the basis not of a few extremists who misuse their faith for sinister purposes, but of the true teachings of the faith and the lives of the vast majority of those who practice it. When that is done, neither Christianity nor Islam should be denounced as violent.

It is, however, crucial not to forget that if it is attacked, Islam can turn very violent in obedience to the Qur'an and Muhammad's example and teachings. This is what causes so much controversy about the use of violence in Islam. It exists in contrast to all the peaceful injunctions of Islam and causes Muslims to react violently to open attacks on their faith.[4]

PRAYING THE PRINCIPLE

Lord, help us to reach out to Muslims in love, patience, humility and un-

derstanding, and bring them to the knowledge of the only true God and his Son, Jesus Christ.

> The LORD tests the righteous and the wicked,
> And the one who loves violence His soul hates. (Psalm 11:5)

If a prophet or a dreamer of dreams arises among you and gives you a sign or a wonder, and the sign or wonder comes true, concerning which he spoke to you, saying, "Let us go after other gods (whom you have not known) and let us serve them," you shall not listen to the words of that prophet or that dreamer of dreams; for the LORD your God is testing you to find out if you love the LORD your God with all your heart and with all your soul. (Deuteronomy 13:1-3)

DISCUSSING THE PRINCIPLE

1. Did Islam begin as a violent religion? If so, why?

2. What is the doctrine of the Greater and Lesser Jihad? How do Muslims live that out?

3. What did Muhammad teach about how to treat unbelievers who don't attack the Islamic faith?

4. What are the four alleged evidences that America is attacking Islam according to some Muslim extremists? What are many Muslim youth taught about America?

5. Do most Muslims live out their faith peacefully or violently? Why?

6. What is the final goal of the Muslim extremists and how do they hope to accomplish it?

19

Are People Who Have Never Heard the Gospel or Who Believe in Other Religions Going to Hell?

Stacie had been in all of my classes. One colleague called her one of my "groupies." She was a very intelligent and likeable young woman who had rejected the Christian faith of her parents because, as she put it, "God just isn't fair." Her point of contention was how God could condemn the majority of human beings to an everlasting hell when most of them had never even heard the gospel and therefore never had a chance to believe in Christ. "Can you please explain that to me?" she challenged. I took her to Romans 1–2.

ROMANS 1–2 AND UNIVERSAL CONDEMNATION

In the first two chapters of Romans Paul is laying the groundwork for his presentation of the good news of the gospel. He starts out explaining the "bad news" first. The bad news is that we are all justly condemned to hell by God for our many sins. To prove that, Paul launches into a threefold argument.

1. Paul explains that all people are responsible for honoring God and giving thanks to him because "since the creation of the world His invisible attributes, His eternal power and divine nature, have been clearly seen, being understood through what has been

made, so they are without excuse" (Romans 1:20). Observing creation should convince anyone that there is a divine being behind it who is incredibly powerful. Paul states, however, that people "suppress the truth" because of their sinfulness (v. 18). Although observing creation should be more than enough to convince them that God exists and that he is powerful, their minds are clouded with illogical arguments against the existence of God, and they build an alternate universe that excludes the necessity of God. They refuse to come to the right conclusion for fear that it will interfere with their sinful and prideful lifestyle (Romans 1:18-19). After all, if there is such a being, he may well have a claim on our obedience and submission, something they want to avoid at any cost. So, Paul continues, God's wrath is "revealed from heaven against all ungodliness and unrighteousness" (Romans 1:18). So, first, all people stand justly under the condemnation of God if they refuse to acknowledge him (Romans 1:28) in spite of what the creation clearly reveals.

2. Paul targets those who know the law of God but don't obey it. He says that "all who have sinned under the Law will be judged by the Law" (Romans 2:12). He argues that it is not enough to hear the law, we must obey it to be justified before God. Later in the passage he insists that "by the works of the Law no flesh will be justified in His sight" because no one can fully obey the law (Romans 3:20). People who try to deserve God's approval by living a perfect life are fooling themselves—no one can do that.

3. Paul writes about those who do not know God's law. He concludes that "all who have sinned without the Law will also perish without the Law" (Romans 2:12). He states that even though non-Jews do not know God's Word, they often

> do instinctively the things of the Law, these [Gentiles], not having the Law, are a law to themselves, in that they show the work of the Law written in their hearts, their conscience bearing witness and their thoughts alternately accusing or else de-

fending them, on the day when, according to my gospel, God will judge the secrets of men [and women] through Christ Jesus. (Romans 2:14-16)

Those who have never heard the Word of God still have a conscience, placed in them by God, which guides them about right and wrong. Their conscience, which is God's law, is "written in their hearts" by God. Those who refuse to live according to the dictates of their conscience will find their own "conscience bearing witness" against them and their thoughts accusing them when they stand before God on judgment day. So, even if people don't know the Word of God and his teachings, they are still responsible to obey the sense of right and wrong, the conscience, that God has placed in them. Violating one's conscience brings judgment before God.

THE POSSIBILITY OF SALVATION WITHOUT FAITH IN CHRIST?

Some of my students have brightened up when I discuss the conscience and ask, "If that is true, can people be saved by obeying their consciences?" My answer has always been, "Well, theoretically, yes. If people fully obeyed the promptings of their consciences, then their consciences would defend them on the day of judgment." However, I always add, "Let's look at how easy or hard that would be." I propose that a certain group of people, let's say a tribe in Africa, have only three proscriptions according to their consciences: do not lie, do not steal, and do not have sex with another person's spouse. All human beings are made in the image of God, so when we live together, we soon discover that lying to one another or stealing from one another or having sex with someone else's spouse is counterproductive—those behaviors produce distrust, suspicion, anger and hatred. Then I ask the class, "If those were the only three things your conscience knew to be wrong, how many of you would have a perfectly clear conscience today?" No hands have ever gone up. Mine has always remained down too.

God has set up his moral universe in such a way that (1) his existence and power are self-evident in nature; (2) he expects people to acknowledge and seek him; (3) the conscience he has placed in every person informs us that there are certain things we should not do, but we do them anyway; therefore (4) we all stand justly condemned before God, whether we have heard the gospel or not, because our own consciences will accuse us before God on the day of judgment. So, those who have never heard the gospel will be judged by God according to their consciences, which will either accuse or defend them before God.

Irish missionary Amy Carmichael had an amazing ministry in India for fifty-five years, rescuing young girls from forced prostitution in Hindu temples. Before she died in 1951, Amy wrote a book titled *Mimosa*, revealing the true story about an Indian woman who heard of God's love as a child. All of her life, she faithfully sought after God, without a church or a Bible or any fellow believers. Mimosa was scorned and persecuted for her faith in that unknown God, but she never wavered in her beliefs. She followed her conscience and the God she loved and served without knowing his name. When the gospel was presented to Mimosa, she joyfully recognized that Jesus was the one she had been worshiping all of her life. She is an example of a person who faithfully followed her conscience without actually knowing the gospel. My brother-in-law, Jerry Daniels, has been a missionary in Kenya for more than thirty-five years. He has shared with me that there are hundreds of Mimosa-type stories that come out of the African bush. People seek God with all their heart, and God finds a way to get the gospel to them, which they recognize as what they have been seeking all their lives.

Those who have never heard the gospel or who have put their faith in another religion without knowing about the gospel will be fairly and justly judged by God according to whether they followed their consciences. This judgment is fair and just, but it is also severe. How many of us could possibly withstand it? That's why missionaries are so important. They proclaim the good news that if we put our trust in Jesus Christ and his atonement on the cross, we can be saved, whether our consciences are clean or not. That good news is the answer to the bad news of universal condemnation and judgment that we all must face without faith in Christ.

After my presentation, Stacie erupted, "Why didn't anybody ever tell me that? If they had told me that I would have never left the church! That's fair! It makes sense." Stacie has still not come to Christ, but she has attended our church a few times when I have preached, and I have great hope for her.

PRAYING THE PRINCIPLE

Lord, you reached me when my conscience was totally defiled. I couldn't tell right from wrong, truth from falsehood, good from bad. If you hadn't touched my life, I would have self-destructed in sin and depravity. How can I ever thank you enough for your grace and your mercy? I give you all of me, and I ask you to help me to keep my conscience clear before you so that I can live in the joy and the power of the abundant life you have promised to give me.

> To the pure, all things are pure; but to those who are defiled and unbelieving, nothing is pure, but both their mind and their conscience are defiled. (Titus 1:15)

DISCUSSING THE PRINCIPLE

1. What was Stacie's problem with Christianity? Do you know people who share her problem?

2. What are Paul's three arguments in Romans 1–2 about why all people are justly condemned by God for their sins? Is that hard for you to accept? Why or why not?

3. Can people be saved by obeying their consciences? What is the problem with that possibility?

4. What are the four elements of the moral universe God has created?

5. What does the example of Mimosa teach us?

6. Why is it so important to send missionaries throughout the world with the good news? Do you believe that those who have never heard the gospel or those who believe in other religions will be condemned by God for not believing in Jesus? Why or why not?

20

What's So Important
About Jesus?

It's always enlightening to hear someone who knows nothing about Christianity respond to a presentation of its basic truths. The tenets of Christianity are so familiar to most of us that we are surprised by the shock they cause in people who hear them for the first time. At the end of my presentation on Christianity in my religion class, Jessica, a smart, young woman, raised her hand and asked, "What's so important about Jesus anyway?" She explained that she had understood his importance in the Christian faith, but wondered what difference that makes in the light of so many world religions with their counterclaims, conflicting doctrines and outstanding leaders. I think that is a valid question.

THE AMAZING UNIQUENESS OF CHRIST

If the claims of Christianity are true, then Jesus is the most amazing, the most unique, the most extraordinary person in all of human history. It's almost as if an alien had come to earth with unbelievable powers and an overwhelming love for human beings. Of course, Jesus is not an alien; he is the Son of God, God in the flesh. So, it's no wonder that the claims of the Christian faith are an intellectual bombshell for those who have never heard them. This truth came home to me when I talked to a hotel staff member in Cuba. I asked him what he knew about Jesus. His response shocked me, "What's his last name?" He honestly knew nothing about Jesus Christ. He had grown up under Castro's regime and had never heard one thing about Jesus. As I shared with him the love, self-sacrifice and power of Jesus, his eyes glistened with amazement. I pray that seed took root.

LIAR, LUNATIC OR LORD

One of the most helpful ways of approaching the question of Jesus' identity was proposed by C. S. Lewis in his outstanding book *Mere Christianity*. Published in 1952, Lewis's book is composed of scripts from his BBC radio broadcasts on the Christian faith. In it Lewis develops what has come to be called the "Liar, Lunatic or Lord" argument about the identity of Jesus. I'll let Lewis speak for himself:

> I am trying here to prevent anyone saying the really foolish thing that people often say about Him: "I'm ready to accept Jesus as a great moral teacher, but I don't accept His claim to be God." That is the one thing we must not say. A man who said the sort of things Jesus said would not be a great moral teacher. He would either be a lunatic—on a level with the man who says he is a poached egg—or else he would be the Devil of Hell. You must make your choice. Either this man was, and is, the Son of God: or else a madman or something worse. You can shut Him up for a fool, you can spit at Him and kill Him as a demon; or you can fall at His feet and call Him Lord and God. But let us not come with any patronizing nonsense about His being a great human teacher. He has not left that open to us. He did not intend to.
>
> We are faced, then, with a frightening alternative. This man we are talking about either was (and is) just what He said, or else a lunatic, or something worse. Now it seems to me obvious that He was neither a lunatic nor a fiend: and consequently, however strange or terrifying or unlikely it may seem, I have to accept the view that He was and is God. God has landed on this enemy-occupied world in human form.[1]

I strongly agree with Lewis that Jesus did not leave any alternative but to accept him as who he said he is—the Lord, the Son of God, God in the flesh—or dismiss him totally as either a monumental fraud or a deluded maniac. Jesus made what some would call outrageous claims about himself. He said that if people had seen him, they had seen God the Father (John 14:8-9). He said, "I and the Father are one" (John 10:30). His Jewish opponents recognized what he was affirming and tried to stone him to death because, they said, "You, being a man, make Yourself out *to be* God" (John 10:33). He claimed to have existed before the patriarch Abraham, and made the claim using the Old Testament designation for God, "I am" (John 8:56-58). Jesus said that he is "the resurrection and the life" (John 11:25). He professed to have the power to forgive sins, and showed his mastery over nature, disease, demons and death itself. He claimed to be "the way, and the truth, and the life," and insisted that no one could come to God the Father except through him (John 14:6). He promised his disciples that he would prepare a place for them in his Father's house (John 14:1-3); and he allowed Thomas to worship him as "My Lord and my God" (John 20:26-29). Surely, these are not the statements and actions of a "good moral teacher." They are either the ravings of a lunatic, the deceit of a pathological liar or the honest self-identifications of the Lord, the Son of God.

THE UNIQUENESS OF JESUS' RESURRECTION

The other factor that makes Jesus unique among all the religious leaders of the world is his resurrection from the dead. Many religious leaders have taught great lessons about life, but none of them, other than Jesus, came back from the dead to live in their followers and help them live out that life. Moses, Muhammad, Buddha, Confucius and the apostle Paul are all dead and buried. Only Jesus has come back from the dead to live in those who put their trust in him. That is why Paul says that Jesus "was declared the Son of God with power by the resurrection from the dead" (Romans 1:4). No other figure in history can make that claim. It is the undeniable demonstration that

Jesus is the most unique, amazing and astounding individual who has ever set foot on planet earth.

PRAYING THE PRINCIPLE

Lord, how can I ever praise you enough? Your love, your mercy, your generosity, your humility, your grace all cry out for you to be honored and glorified and magnified above all things, all people, all creation. I praise you with every ounce of my being, and my one great desire is to be with you so that I can praise you face to face in all of your glory for ever and ever!

"Worthy is the Lamb that was slain to receive power and riches
    and wisdom and might and honor and glory and
    blessing."
And every created thing . . . I heard saying,
    "To Him who sits on the throne, and to the Lamb, *be* blessing
    and honor and glory and dominion forever and ever."
And the four living creatures kept saying, "Amen." And the
    elders fell down and worshiped. (Revelation 5:12-14)

DISCUSSING THE PRINCIPLE

1. Why are Christianity's claims about Jesus so startling to unbelievers?

2. Summarize C. S. Lewis's argument that Jesus is either Lord, lunatic or demon. What do you think of that argument?

3. What are some of the outrageous things that Jesus did and said?

4. What is unique about Jesus' resurrection and his relationship with his followers? How does that fact make him absolutely matchless among world religious leaders?

5. How would you now answer someone who asked you why Jesus is so important?

PART FIVE

Questions About Contemporary Controversies

Christians must deal with some of the major issues that confront us in modern society, especially those that tend to make non-Christians resistant to the gospel. Although we can't possibly be experts on every issue that arises, we can clearly express our Christian point of view in the face of many of the concerns that people have about life. Not only do we need to be able to share our understanding about these issues, but we need to know how to respond to the challenges of modern society and live consistently and knowledgeably as Christians.

One of the incredible things about God's Word is that the more questions we ask of it, the more answers we find in it. Until recently we didn't need to ask what the Bible taught about evolution because the theory of evolution did not yet exist. But now that it does, we must seek Scripture's answers for our contemporary situation.

In this final section, we will consider five modern issues that to some extent challenge and call into question our Christian faith:

1. Are science and the Bible contradictory, and is one superior to the other?

2. Is it possible for Christians to accept both the Bible and the theory of evolution without compromising their faith or rejecting respected scientific knowledge?

3. Do biblical prohibitions against premarital sex still hold?

4. What is the Bible's view of unborn children and a mother's right to abortion?

5. Does the Bible condemn homosexuality, or is homosexuality a valid lifestyle?

The answers to these concerns will both inform our faith and enable us to communicate it better to those outside of it. Christianity must be true to Scripture and relevant to the new issues cropping up in modern society.

21

Do Science and the Bible
Contradict Each Other?

I was first asked whether science and the Bible contradict each other many years ago at the University of Iowa. About four hundred students gathered for a question-and-answer session. A pre-med student, Robert, said, "I am studying science and I am a Christian. But it seems that the more science I study, the harder it is to accept what the Bible says. Don't they contradict each other?" I sensed his anxiety. Do you have to give up the Bible to commit yourself to science? I don't think so.

HOT DOGS AND SCIENCE

I told those students the story of the little boy who came into the kitchen and saw some water boiling on the stove. He asked, "Dad, why is that water boiling?" "Well, son, the heat in the burner makes the molecules in the water go faster and faster until they finally turn into steam. That's what makes water boil," his father responded. "Thanks, Dad," the boy said with obvious frustration. He went into the bedroom and asked his mother, "Why is the water boiling on the stove?" She answered, "Because we're having hot dogs for lunch."

Both of those answers are true. It's just that one is scientific and one is *teleological* (a fancy word for expressing purpose). Science and the Bible are like that. They offer different kinds of answers to people's questions, but both answers are valuable. The Bible deals more with faith, morality, God and the afterlife; while science deals more with observable facts, natural systems and cause-and-effect relationships. Science has its realm, and the Bible has another, and the two don't often intersect, but sometimes they do. How do we deal with those intersections?

Christianity and the scientific community have had a troubled history in the past. At one time early scientists thought life was created through "spontaneous generation." This was based on the observation that when meat is left in the open for days, maggots appear—"spontaneous production of life." Well, that was not science's finest hour! On the other hand, the Roman Catholic Church found Galileo "vehemently suspect of heresy" in 1633 for suggesting that the earth is not the center of the universe. That was not Christianity's finest hour either. Through the years, science and Christianity have had an uneasy relationship produced in part by some scientists' desire to rid the world of "religious superstition" and in part by some Christians' assumption that modern science is "of the devil." Fortunately, neither description is accurate.

MIRACLES AND SCIENCE

One of the big problems between science and Christianity is that most Christians insist that miracles really do happen. Traditionally, Christians believe Moses parted the Red Sea, and Jesus walked on water, healed ill people, raised people from the dead, and was resurrected himself. (Admittedly, some Christians have abandoned belief in biblical miracles, fearing that it makes the Christian faith unacceptable to modern society.)

One of the best advocates for belief in miracles has been C. S. Lewis. In his book *Miracles*, Lewis has a fascinating discussion of the supposed conflict between miracles and the laws of nature. Many scientists believe that the laws of nature cannot be violated. The essence of science is the assumption that everything can be explained from natural causes without resorting to supernatural actions by any divine being. Lewis counters that claim by insisting that

1. All of nature is actually supernatural since it was all created by a supernatural God.

2. The laws of nature are actually not laws at all; they are descriptions of the way things usually happen. That does not exclude the possibility that, at times, things don't happen in the usual ways.

3. Since the laws of nature do not cause things to happen (they merely record what usually happens), they can't possibly prevent something unusual from taking place.

4. Miracles don't break the laws of nature; the laws are suspended momentarily. Then they go back to the normal way established by God.

5. Both the laws of nature and miracles are works of the same God. Science is an attempt to discover how God ordered nature in his creation, and miracles are occurrences that illustrate God's ability to intervene in his creation to do something new and unique. Both are acts of the one God!

Surely science and faith can walk hand in hand as together we contemplate the wonder, beauty and magnificence of what God has done! Good science and good faith are never in conflict. They both serve the same God. We discover God's thoughts about nature by studying its intricacies; Scripture communicates God's wonderful plan for human beings. Remember, both *scientific heat transference* and *cooking hot dogs for lunch* explain why the water is boiling on the stove![1]

PRAYING THE PRINCIPLE

You are a miracle-working God, and I praise you for your mastery over all the forces of nature. I long to see more and more of your miraculous power in and through my life today.

> How will we escape if we neglect so great a salvation? After it was at the first spoken through the Lord, it was confirmed to us by those who heard, God also testifying with them, both by signs and wonders and by various miracles and by gifts of the Holy Spirit according to His own will. (Hebrews 2:3-4)

DISCUSSING THE PRINCIPLE

1. How does the "boiling water" story illustrate the differences between science and the Bible?

2. Give examples of some of the struggles between science and Christianity. What attitudes were often behind those conflicts? Are they necessary? How can they be avoided?

3. Why have miracles been such a problem for many scientists?

4. Summarize C. S. Lewis's five points on miracles and the "laws of nature." Do you agree with him? Why or why not?

5. How can science and faith walk hand-in-hand?

22

Can a Christian Believe in Evolution?

John came to my office with a worried face. He asked, "Can I believe in evolution and still be a Christian?" I responded, "What brought this on, John?" He shared how his anthropology professor had attacked a student in his class for believing in the Bible. "He told us that the Bible is full of myths and that evolution has proven that no God created the world. He said the world came into existence on its own, and then the process of evolution produced everything we see today in nature. I don't know what to think anymore."

Many college and high school students struggle with this question (as do many adults). When confronted with what seems to be the overwhelming evidence for evolution in many science courses, they have two options: throw away their faith as nothing more than a collection of unscientific myths, or hide their heads in the sand of "religious fanaticism" and ignore the scientific evidence. Fortunately, those are not the only two choices available to Christians.

EVOLUTION AND SCIENTISTS' PRESUPPOSITIONS

It would actually be more accurate to ask, Can a Christian *accept* evolution? since a scientific theory does not really lend itself to belief or unbelief. Unfortunately, a great deal of modern science asks for dogmatic acceptance rather than objective evaluation of its views and theories. Too often scientists' conclusions are based on their own presuppositions and prejudices with a veneer of science painted over them. In many cases evolutionist scientists have crossed the line from science to philosophy in their conclusions. Rather than follow the scientific method of question-observation-hypothesis-experimentation-conclusion, they have allowed their antisupernatural philosophical bias, instead of the facts, to determine their conclusions. If someone doesn't believe God exists, some other plausible explanation for the origin of the universe and its incredible diversity has to be devised. But Christians have other objections to the theory of evolution.

CHRISTIAN OBJECTIONS TO EVOLUTION

The following are aspects of evolutionary theory that a Christian cannot accept.

1. Atheistic evolution. That life randomly popped into existence from nothing can neither be proved nor disproved by science. It is an illogical assumption in the light of the complexity, beauty and interconnectedness of the creation. As Norman Geisler says, "I don't have enough faith to be an atheist." All attempts to explain the origin of the universe without God lead to questions like, Where did that come from? A Russian scientist has suggested that the universe began from a primal material called "xylem." But the question still stands, Where did the xylem come from? He has no answer. Only God, the Uncaused Cause, can finally answer that question satisfactorily. Everything came from God, who spoke all matter into existence. He has no beginning. He is infinite and not caused by anything or anyone else. Atheistic evolution is a theory with no real foundation or logic. Obviously, as Christians we cannot accept it.

2. Species arise gradually from mutations in lower species. Darwinian evolution teaches that over millions of years small beneficial mutations (micromutations) made some animals better able to survive and reproduce more offspring in their environment than other animals could. After many generations those changes are established and there is a new species. For example, evolution posits that among giraffe-like creatures with short necks, grazing plants became scarce, so those born with unusually long necks were able to eat leaves from the treetops, survive better and produce more offspring. After many generations the long neck feature became dominant. The result: modern-day giraffes. This "survival of the fittest" (or "natural selection") is the engine that drives the evolutionary process. However, this is a weak point of evolution when it is applied to changes between species.

First, the fossil record does not show evidence of gradual change from one species to another. It shows gaps between species. Most biology textbooks illustrate this fact by placing dotted lines between species. Darwin recognized this weakness, but hoped that future generations would find evidence of the incredible number of "missing links" that his theory requires. But that has not happened. The fossil record does not show the millions of examples of gradual changes between species that evolution requires to be proven true.

Second, the idea of successful, gradual changes from one species to another presupposes that those changes would be beneficial and that the new, "fittest" animal would survive and procreate more. But a simple example reveals the problem of this theory. The change from reptiles to birds requires the transformation of legs into wings, but the gradual changes needed for this change to occur do not produce a superior animal. When an animal is born with 75 percent leg and 25 percent wing, it cannot fly and it can no longer run as fast as those with fully formed legs. It is no longer the fittest. As the required change progresses, it becomes increasingly harmful. A 50 percent leg and 50 percent wing appendage is disastrous for the animal. Gradual change simply does not work to produce radical, beneficial changes between species.

The only other option is "macromutations" (emergent evolution), which proposes that a lizard egg produced a bird. This idea is nothing short of ridiculous. Nothing like it has ever been observed in nature. It just shows how desperate some evolutionists are to account for the lack of transitional forms in the fossil record and the unproductive results of championing micromutations between species. Emergent evolutionists have produced volumes exposing the weaknesses of traditional Darwinian evolution, but they are likewise hard-pressed to produce any evidence for what they propose.

THE BIBLE AND EVOLUTIONARY THEORY

God's Word says that God caused animals to reproduce "after their kind" (Genesis 1:20-25). This agrees with the gaps found in the fossil record. According to Genesis, different kinds of animals came into being by God's creative word and reproduced according to their kind. However, there is one element of evolutionary theory that complements the biblical record—variation. Animals change *within* their species or kind through survival of the fittest. For example, there was a time in England when most peppered moths were light in color, though a minority of them were darker. The lighter ones were able to blend into the light-colored lichens and tree barks they rested on, and they flourished. But after the Industrial Revolution hit England, pollution killed off most of the lichens and turned the tree barks a darker color. Soon the darker moths became the dominant expression of peppered moths in England because it was easier for them to blend in and avoid predators. The moths that survived best became the dominant form of that species of moth. Variation works *within* species (kinds), but not *between* species. As we have seen, gradual changes between species are not beneficial.

SUMMARY OF A CHRISTIAN VIEW OF EVOLUTION

Can a Christian accept evolution? The answer is yes and no. Thinking Christians cannot accept the ideas of evolution that contradict the fossil record, violate evolution's own principle of survival of the fittest and conflict with God's Word. But we can accept variation within species because it is an observable fact in nature and it offers an explanation for the varieties of animals within each *kind* that God created. While there is great variation *within* species, they do not evolve into other species. However, it appears that God uses variation within his creation to help animals adapt to changing environments and continually improve. In my neighborhood there is a Chihuahua at one end of the block and a huge lion dog at the other, but they are both dogs, and their offspring will be dogs too.

I once confronted Cliff, a biologist studying bats in Costa Rica, with some of the problems in the theory of evolution. After his attempts to defend evolution, he finally stood up and shouted, "If I listened to you, it would destroy the whole basis of my life and my work!" With that outburst, Cliff left the house. I had touched a nerve that he could not tolerate. Evolutionists live and work in a very precarious house of cards that can easily collapse if they are honest and open enough to consider it objectively.[1]

PRAYING THE PRINCIPLE

Lord, I praise you for your creation. Its beauty, awesomeness and majesty are unmistakable evidences of your intelligence, your power and your love for us. You could have made us live in a drab, lifeless world, but you surrounded our lives with beauty and surprise at every turn. The flowers and the animals are constant reminders of your greatness and your generosity. Thank you.

> Then God said, "Let the earth bring forth living creatures after their kind: cattle and creeping things and beasts of the earth after their kind"; and it was so. (Genesis 1:24)

> By faith we understand that the worlds were prepared by the word of God, so that which is seen was not made out of things which are visible. (Hebrews 11:3)

DISCUSSING THE PRINCIPLE

1. What are the false choices people make when confronted with the evidence for evolution?

2. Why is it hard to accept some scientists' conclusions as objective when their science seems to serve their philosophical positions?

3. Summarize the two arguments against the gradual changes that would produce one species from another. What is your opinion about this?

4. How does what the Bible says about the development of animals fit with the fossil record and changes that occur *inside* species of animals, not *between* them?

5. What is variation and how does it successfully tie together good science and God's Word?

6. What is your opinion: Can Christians accept evolution? Explain.

23

Is Premarital Sex Still Wrong?

When I talk to my classes about God's will and the destructiveness of sin, they inevitably bring up premarital sex as an example of a "good sin." They often ask, as a young woman named Debbie put it, "I don't see how having sex before marriage can be wrong. It's the best way to find out if two people are compatible, and it's fun. Why is God such a prude?" I assured Debbie that God is not a prude; he created sex for our enjoyment and for reproduction. After all, God could have created us to produce babies by rubbing noses or ears or elbows! But he chose to give us the great physical pleasure of sex for our delight and for producing children. They look puzzled at this, and usually one will ask something like, "If God is so high on sex, why does he tell us not to do it? We can avoid unwanted pregnancies now."

PREMARITAL SEX IS CONDEMNED

The Bible does not prohibit premarital sex because of the fear of unwanted pregnancies. However, there *are* valid reasons why premarital sex is not good. First, let's establish clearly that the Bible unequivocally prohibits premarital sexual relations (fornication) and extramarital sexual relations (adultery). In the New Testament alone, fornication is condemned in Acts 15:20, 29; Romans 1:24; 1 Corinthians 5:11; 6:13-18; 10:8; Galatians 5:19; Ephesians 5:3; Colossians 3:5; 1 Thessalonians 4:3; and Jude 7. Why all the fuss? Apparently, this is a big deal to God. He wants the very best for our lives, so let's explore some of the possible reasons why premarital sex is destructive.

1. Something mystical and eternal happens when people have sex. In 1 Corinthians 6, Paul makes several points about the problem of premarital (or extramarital) sex:

- "the body is not for immorality, but for the Lord, and the Lord is for the body" (v. 13)

- "your bodies are members of Christ" and should not be joined to someone who is not your spouse (v. 15)

- when you join your body with someone in sex, you are "one body" with that person (v. 16)

- the one who commits immorality "sins against his own body" (v. 18)

- "your body is a temple of the Holy Spirit who is in you" (v. 19)

- "Do you not know that . . . you are not your own? For you have been bought with a price: therefore glorify God in your body" (vv. 19-20).

Wow! That pretty much says it all, doesn't it? Our bodies belong to the Lord, and we are not to join our bodies to someone who is not our husband or wife.

Unfortunately, many people don't follow Paul's advice and end up suffering for it. If you date someone without having sex and then break up, you go on with your life—no problem. But if you have had sex with someone and then break up, you experience something like a minidivorce each time that happens. The human psyche was not created to take that much emotional abuse without serious and long-lasting consequences.

2. Premarital sex causes a couple to focus on the physical in their relationship. Premarital sex detours couples from the vital need to get to know each other's heart, mind, will, goals, preferences, opinions and dreams. Many couples who have made sex a major part of their relationship discover after they get married that they don't know each other well. Experiencing sex too soon in a relationship makes it difficult to have the kind of communication and sharing needed for a successful marriage.

3. Premarital sex is dangerous because of sexually transmitted disease. It has been said that when you have sex with someone, you are having sex with every other person with whom that person has had sex. Someone can have sex with one person, one time, and the result can be death! AIDS, genital herpes, gonorrhea, syphilis, chlamydia and a host of other problems can be contracted from sex with the wrong person—just one time. Is it worth the risk?

4. Birth control as an absolute guarantee against unwanted pregnancy is an illusion. No birth control method, including the pill, is 100 percent effective. Many women find themselves pregnant even though they think they have taken all the necessary precautions to avoid a pregnancy. Many couples intend on using a condom, but sometimes, in the heat of the moment, those great intentions fly out the window. Besides, condoms don't always work. Birth control is not a sure thing.

5. Premarital sex produces trust issues after marriage. Often, when one's spouse has had multiple sexual partners before marriage, the person wonders whether he or she will be satisfied with just one sexual relationship after marriage. A spouse who was unable to practice sexual discipline before marriage may be prone not to practice sexual discipline after marriage either. Multiple partners also open the door to uncomfortable comparisons that can damage a marital relationship. Hearing your spouse say after sex, "That was good, but you know, so-and-so does it better," is not conducive to marital bliss, harmony and self-esteem! Sometimes that kind of comparison is unexpressed, but it nonetheless breeds dissatisfaction in the marriage relationship, which is also destructive.

6. Memories of previous sexual partners create temptation once a person is married. Memories of previous sexual encounters never go away, and seeing a former sexual partner can trigger strong feelings and increase the temptation to be unfaithful to one's spouse. Marriage today is complicated enough and susceptible to enough problems without allowing sexual memories to dog your married life.

7. *Premarital sex robs people of the joy of experiencing the pleasures of sex together for the first time on their wedding night.* I have often asked my students, "What was your first sexual experience like?" Time and again they have answered, "Horrible, scary, nasty, painful, clumsy, awful." Many times it has happened in places where they could have easily been discovered, and they were afraid. Frequently, young women share that they were talked into it as a "proof of love," but the guy dumped them afterward. That kind of manipulative, hurried, secretive, frightening experience is not what God has planned for the initiation of our sexual relations. In God's eyes, sex has been given to us to be enjoyed by two virgins—with no shame, no fear, no hiding.

THE ECSTASY OF PREMARITAL VIRGINITY!

My wife and I were both virgins when we married. It was the greatest physical thrill of our lives to discover the joy of sex together for the first time. (I can feel her blushing now as she reads this!) What an ecstasy, with no baggage from the past and the pure joy of learning to please each other more and more! That is God's best for every couple, and I long to see more young people experience that joy as they promise to wait until marriage! As one of the more popular youth movements today affirms, "It's great to wait!"

PRAYING THE PRINCIPLE

Lord, thank you for the way you designed us to experience such ecstatic pleasure when we make love to one another. Your plan is wonderful! Please help us to keep that desire under control and save our most intimate sexual experience for our wedding night so that we can enjoy the full satisfaction and exhilaration that you have planned for us.

> You know what commandments we gave you by *the authority of*
> the Lord Jesus. For this is the will of God, your sanctification;
> *that is*, that you abstain from sexual immorality; that each of

you know how to possess his own vessel in sanctification and honor, not in lustful passion, like the Gentiles who do not know God. (1 Thessalonians 4:2-5)

DISCUSSING THE PRINCIPLE

1. Is God a prude about sex? Explain.

2. Summarize the seven reasons given why premarital sex is destructive of God's best for our lives. Share personal experiences of your own and of people you know that illustrate each point.

3. Why does God desire wedding night sex between two virgins? Are you committed to that vision?

24

What Does the Bible
Teach About Abortion?

For several years I taught a college course titled "Religion and Contemporary Society," in which I brought in speakers from varied backgrounds to speak to my students. One of the topics we looked at was abortion. I always invited a representative of Care Net, a Christian crisis pregnancy program, and also a representative of Planned Parenthood. They presented their views to the students in successive class meetings, and then I led a discussion with the class on abortion. The discussion was always heated, with some students strongly asserting a woman's right to an abortion and others arguing for the protection of the unborn child. That's what makes this such a difficult issue—it pits two good things against each other. The right of women to control their own bodies and the right of unborn children to live are both good, but one has to prevail over the other in this conflict of interests.

CARE NET VERSUS PLANNED PARENTHOOD

Over time, one of the things I observed in class was how similar the two speakers were in some ways. They both cared about women and their problems. They both wanted to see fewer abortions—one by stopping all of them and the other by giving sex education classes to help women avoid unwanted pregnancies. They both connected with my students and seemed sincerely interested in helping them deal with these difficult issues.

But that's where the similarities ended. The Care Net presenter stressed the needs of the unborn child; the Planned Parenthood presenter centered on the needs of the woman. In fact, the Planned Parenthood rep often referred to the unborn child as either "the product of conception," "tissue" or "the fetus." The Care Net rep showed us plastic models of the developing unborn child and shared a DVD on the methods of abortion, which was very disturbing to the class. It wasn't gory or sensationalistic, but it clearly described what happens to the unborn baby during an abortion. Students cringed as the doctor described in a matter-of-fact way that during an abortion the unborn child is burned, torn apart or has its skull collapsed. Many of my students had no idea what is done to a baby in an abortion, and most of them were appalled.

Every time the presentation was made, there were tears in at least one young woman's eyes as she finally realized what she had allowed someone to do to her baby. My heart went out to those students. Many of them had not been told there were viable alternatives to abortion when they experienced an unwanted pregnancy. The Care Net communicator was very kind and understanding, and emphasized that Care Net does not judge women; they help them instead. In fact, they offer postabortion counseling for those who have already aborted a child and are suffering the aftereffects. The Planned Parenthood rep insisted that most women have no trauma after having an abortion, only relief. Many of my female students who had gone through an abortion contradicted that view in their discussions with her. But a few of them agreed with her. The view that the unborn child is not really a person also prompted some very heated discussions.

THE BIBLE AND UNBORN CHILDREN

So, what does the Bible say about unborn children—are they humans or just the "product of conception" or "tissue" in the woman's body over which she has absolute control? Well, in fact, the Bible does not say a great deal about this topic. There are, however, seven key passages that shed light on God's views on prebirth children.

Exodus 21:22-23. "If men struggle with each other and strike a woman so that she gives birth prematurely, yet there is no injury, he shall surely be fined as the woman's husband may demand of him, and he shall pay as the judges *decide.* But if there is *any further* injury, then you shall appoint *as a penalty* life for life." The unborn child is a human and if two men fight and cause the child to be born prematurely and the child dies, the one who injured the mother is punished with death. Just yesterday I heard on the news of a drive-by shooting in which a pregnant woman was killed. The shooter was charged with two murders—hers and the unborn child's. The pre-birth child is a human and must be protected as such.

Job 31:15. "Did not He who made me in the womb make him [a slave], / And the same one fashion us in the womb?" God makes people in the womb; they are his *human* creation. They are humans before they are born.

Psalm 139:13. "For You formed my inward parts; / You wove me in my mother's womb." God formed us in the womb and we are "fearfully and wonderfully made" (v. 14). God saw us being formed in our mother's womb and decided how long we would live before we were born. We are humans seen by God and the object of his sovereign will before we are born.

Isaiah 44:24. "Thus says the LORD, your Redeemer, and the one who formed you from the womb . . ." The Lord formed us from the womb. We are humans before we are born.

Judges 13:7. "Behold, you shall conceive and give birth to a son, and now you shall not drink wine or strong drink nor eat any unclean thing, for the boy shall be a Nazirite to God from the womb to the day of his death." Samson was called by God to be a Nazirite "from the womb." God called him as a human before his birth.

Jeremiah 1:5. "Before I formed you in the womb I knew you, / And before you were born I consecrated you; / I have appointed you a prophet to the nations." God called Jeremiah to be a prophet while he was still in his mother's womb, before he was born. He was a prebirth human, called by God.

Galatians 1:15. "God . . . set me apart *even* from my mother's womb and called me through His grace." God called Paul to be an apostle while he was in his mother's womb. He was a human before he was born.

I could give many more examples like these. Suffice it to say that far from seeing prebirth children as "the product of conception" or tissue or a prehuman fetus, God sees them as human beings, as children, who are known, named, called and consecrated by him. God does not relate that way with globs of tissue or material products. He only relates to people, human beings, actual children, who are children before they are born. Anything done to them is done to *children*, not to inhuman blobs. In God's sight, those who kill them are guilty of murder just as if they had killed a four-year-old (see Exodus 21:22-23).

"YES . . . BUT"

Even after studying these biblical teachings about prebirth children, there are still many serious questions. I have called an entire group of these concerns the "yes . . . but" questions. These concerns recognize that the child dies in the abortion, but insist that there are other elements to be considered.

1. What about pregnancies that are the result of incest or rape? Surely a woman should not be expected to give birth to a child of incest or rape, many would say. First, less than 3 percent of the abortions performed in this country are the result of rape or incest. More than 97 percent of US abortions are carried out for *convenience.* Second, should the child be made to suffer for the sins of the father? Granted, carrying such a baby for nine months is emotionally devastating to many women, but isn't being killed for your father's sins much more devastating for the child? Thousands of childless couples desperately want to adopt a child. They could give that child love and care without the stigma of the child's violent conception. Is it too much to ask a woman to bear and birth a child conceived badly if it saves the child's life and offers the child a decent future through adoption? I think not.

2. What if the child is unwanted? Don't many unwanted children suffer terribly and often end up as criminals? Is it better to live "unwanted" or to be killed? Many people who were unwanted at birth grow up to be wonderful people. Rachel, a great friend of ours, was aborted by her mother. A doctor walked through the abortion room and heard her crying. He fished her out of the throw-away tray, took her to the neonatal unit and saved her life. She is one of the best students I have ever taught, was president of a Christian organization on our secular campus, and was a constant source of encouragement, love, counsel and prayer support for multitudes of people. Today, she is a beautiful wife, mother of two great kids and a leader in her church. Being unwanted does not necessarily destroy a person's life. Many children who are unwanted by their birth mothers are desperately wanted and treasured by adoptive parents. Rachel and countless others are living proof that God can turn "unwanted" into "highly valued."

And the argument that unwanted children often turn to crime in later life is wrong on two accounts. First, I know of no reputable research that supports that claim. Second, even' if that claim were proven to be absolutely true, "social engineering" based on possible outcomes is a ghoulish concept that smacks of determinism and inevitability. Christians do not believe that a poor start in life or childhood trauma or parental neglect can determine a bad end for a person. God's grace is more than sufficient to overcome all of those obstacles. As one pro-lifer in England said, "The only crime in England that still carries the death penalty is being unwanted." That is true, and it is wrong!

3. What if giving birth would kill the mother, or the child is terribly deformed? All of us know of cases in which the doctor said the mother would die or the child would be hopelessly handicapped, and that dire prediction has proven to be false. In many of those cases, the mothers survive the birth and the children are born completely healthy. Medical science cannot accurately predict the effect giving birth will have on a mother. Neither can it predict how a deformed prebirth child will develop after being born. Even if the worst happens, do we have the right to take one life to save another, or to take a life to avoid possible future pain and suffering? My wife has made it clear to me that we would never sacrifice a child's life to save hers. We would trust the Lord to save both of them, and receive whatever he decided with love, faith and trust. We have friends who have children with Down syndrome, extreme autism, spina bifida and other problems, but they all are thankful to God for that child, and they love their children with all their hearts. Handicapped children bear the image of God and should be treated with respect, love and gratitude to God.

4. Doesn't a woman have the right to decide what goes on in her own body? Modern legislation has made it clear that one person's rights cannot be used to harm someone else (except in the case of an unborn child). I have a right to "pursue happiness," but *not* if my happiness is found in beating someone and taking all of his or her money. Yes, women have rights, but so do unborn children. Even though our laws now allow women to abort their unborn children, that decision is morally and ethically wrong in God's eyes. Unborn children have rights in God's eyes, and no one has a right to end their lives.

Whatever happened to the self-sacrificing values of motherhood? Are we so self-centered and egotistical that we would rather kill our own children than nurture them for nine months and give them a chance at happiness with another family? As Christians, we affirm that women do have rights, but they do not have the right to kill their own children.

5. Wouldn't making abortions illegal cause women to seek dangerous backstreet abortions? It is difficult for me to understand why any woman would prefer to risk her life with a "backstreet abortionist" rather than carry the child for nine months and give the child up for adoption. At least the woman has that choice. The unborn baby has no choice. In abortions, *the babies die.* They have no say in the matter. Their lives are cut short. Pregnant women have choices. They need to consider their babies when they make them.

ONE FINAL THOUGHT ON ABORTION

How many people have been lost to us because of abortions? Care Net reports that more than fifty million children have been aborted in the United States in the last thirty-six years. Currently, 1.2 million children are being aborted in this country every year. That's 3,288 per day, 137 per hour, 2.3 per minute![1] We will never know what they could have accomplished or how God could have used their lives to improve the world. That is one of the many tragedies of abortion.

This carnage must stop. Children are being sacrificed on the altars of self-fulfillment, convenience and self-centeredness—children that God loves—children that God has sent into this world for a purpose. Years from now people will be appalled that we killed our own young with so little compassion and personal sense of guilt. I pray that God multiplies ministries like Care Net throughout our country to provide viable, safe and effective alternatives to abortion so that we can stem the tide of this terrible epidemic of death.

PRAYING THE PRINCIPLE

Lord, children are such a blessing to all of us. We praise you that you know each of us while we are still in our mothers' wombs. You relate to us as humans before we are born. Help us to protect the innocent, helpless unborn children from the terrible death that awaits many of them in abortion clinics. Lord, please guide Christians to adopt unwanted children and give them a warm, loving home so that their mothers will not be tempted to abort them. Help us to oppose the pro-abortion movement, but support mothers in crisis pregnancies, to your glory.

Behold, children are a gift of the LORD,
The fruit of the womb is a reward.
Like arrows in the hand of a warrior,

So are the children of one's youth.
How blessed is the man whose quiver is full of them.
(Psalm 127:3-5)

DISCUSSING THE PRINCIPLE

1. What makes abortion such a difficult issue?

2. What were the similarities between the representatives of Care Net and Planned Parenthood?

3. What were the differences between the presentations of the Care Net and Planned Parenthood representatives?

4. Summarize the content of the seven biblical passages that deal with the question of whether an unborn child is human. How did those passages affect you? What is your conclusion on this issue of the humanity of unborn children?

5. Summarize the issues and answers involved in the five "yes . . . but" questions. Is that presentation convincing to you? Explain.

6. What is the final argument the author presents against abortion? Has this chapter convinced you of the need to actively oppose abortion? Why or why not? What will you do about it?

25

Is Homosexuality a Sin?

We live in a time of unprecedented tensions between heterosexuals and homosexuals. Just a brief search of the Internet produced the following headlines: "Christian Protest Group Faces 47 Years in Prison," "Christian Student Denied Right to Protest during Homosexual Day," "Homosexual Group to Protest Christian Colleges," "College Professor Fired for Anti-Gay Statements," "VP of University of Toledo Fired for Article Against Gay Rights" and "Christian Ministry Fined $23,000 in Gay Discrimination Case."

Homosexuality became the most controversial and heated topic in my college religion classes. Many students are appalled by any hint that God rejects homosexuals. "After all," one student said, "how can God reject them when he made them that way? People are homosexual from birth; they don't choose it." Other students have tried to uphold the biblical concept of homosexuality as sin, but all too often they have come across in a hateful, arrogant, judgmental way. Homosexual students have been deeply hurt by some of those discussions, despite my best efforts to keep the debates civil. Homosexuality has become one of the touchiest topics in modern American culture.

Is it possible for Christians to objectively consider homosexuality without allowing personal biases and emotions to get in the way? I think so, but it means we must be very careful in interpreting the scriptural passages that deal with this subject, and we must leave our preconceived notions behind as we look at God's Word.

SIX BIBLICAL TEXTS ON BOTH PERSPECTIVES OF HOMOSEXUALITY

There are six main texts about homosexuality in the Bible. Homosexual Christian groups have worked hard dealing with these passages and have come up with some reinterpretations of them that we need to consider. One of the strongest voices in our country for "homosexual Christianity" is the Metropolitan Community Churches (MCC), a denomination headed currently by the Rev. Dr. Nancy Wilson. Founded in 1968, MCC now has over 300 churches in 22 countries with more than 43,000 members. MCC identifies itself as a "GLBT" (Gay, Lesbian, Bisexual and Transgender) church. Although their doctrinal statement mirrors much of evangelical Christianity, the theologians of MCC have gone to great pains to deal with those six biblical passages in their writings.

The Rev. Dr. Mona West, the current pastor of the MCC church in Sarasota, Florida, and a leading theologian in the gay church movement, is the coeditor of *The Queer Bible Commentary* and *Take Back the Word: A Queer Reading of the Bible*. She has also written several short articles and sermons on MCC beliefs, which can be accessed on the MCC website. In one of those, "The Bible and Homosexuality," West addresses the question of what the Bible actually says about homosexuality. She laments that "the Bible is frequently used as a weapon to 'bash' lesbians and gays." She adds that the six passages I have referenced "have been used to justify hatred, condemnation and exclusion of God's lesbian and gay children."[1] I am absolutely against homosexual bashing in any form. There is no excuse for hatred and abuse perpetrated by any Christian against anyone for any reason.

Let's look at the six biblical passages she writes about, consider her take on them and attempt to suggest an evangelical perspective on each one.

THE DESTRUCTION OF SODOM IN GENESIS 19

In Genesis 19:1-29, Lot entertains two angels as visitors in his home. The men of Sodom want Lot to hand over the men to them saying, "'Bring them out to us that we may have relations with them.' But Lot went out to them at the doorway, and shut the door behind him, and said, 'Please, my brothers, do not act wickedly'" (vv. 5-7). When the men tried to force their way into the home, the angels pulled Lot into the home and struck the men blind (vv. 10-11). "Then the LORD rained on Sodom and Gomorrah brimstone and fire" (v. 24). The passage is clear that the men of Sodom wanted to have homosexual relations with the two men. Lot considered their desire to be wicked, and they were blinded for their insistence. There is no clear indication that God decided to destroy the city because of this homosexual incident since the two angels were sent to destroy it before this incident took place. Chapter eighteen simply states that the sin of the people of Sodom and Gomorrah was "exceedingly grave" (v. 20).

West responds that the sin portrayed here is not homosexuality but "rape and inhospitality." She adds that in other biblical passages such as Ezekiel 16:49 and Luke 17:28-29, the sin of Sodom "is not identified as homosexuality, rather their sins were pride, failure to help the poor, and lack of hospitality to foreigners."[2] She dismisses the idea that homosexuality is the cause of God's destruction of the city.

But I would ask, If their desire for homosexual relations with the visitors was not wicked and sinful, then why did the angels blind them? Although there is no clear evidence in the passage itself that the Lord sent the angels to destroy Sodom because of their homosexual conduct, it is certainly clear that the angels sent by God punished the men of Sodom for trying to force the angels to have homosexual relations with them. Moreover, other biblical passages make it clear that God destroyed Sodom because of the inhabitants' sexual perversion (see Jude 7; 2 Peter 2:6-10).

The men of Sodom first asked Lot to bring the visitors out voluntarily to have sex with them, but when Lot knew what they wanted, he branded it as acting "wickedly." Not just the threat of homosexual rape but even the idea of consensual homosexual relations is condemned as wicked. In Ezekiel 16:50, God says that the Sodomites "committed abominations before Me."

In Jude 7 and 2 Peter 2:6-10, the sin of Sodom and Gomorrah is clearly identified as sexual sin. According to Jude, they "indulged in gross immorality and went after strange flesh," and according to 2 Peter, the city was destroyed because of "the sensual conduct of unprincipled men, . . . who indulge the flesh in *its* corrupt desires." God did indeed destroy Sodom because of its inhabitants' homosexual practices and other sins as well.

LEVITICUS PASSAGES

Two Leviticus passages refer to homosexual conduct. In Leviticus 18:22 God commands the Israelites, "You shall not lie with a man as one lies with a female; it is an abomination." In Leviticus 20:13 God announces the punishment for homosexual relations, "If *there is* a man who lies with a male as those who lie with a woman, both of them have committed a detestable act; they shall surely be put to death. Their bloodguiltiness is upon them." Clearly, God considers homosexual relations to be abominable, according to the author of Leviticus.

West, however, explains that "this prohibition in Leviticus was an attempt to preserve the internal harmony of Jewish male society" by stopping them from using homosexual intercourse as a weapon for expressing dominance over other males, as the nations around them did. She insists that "these verses in no way prohibit, nor do they even speak, to loving, caring sexual relationships between people of the same gender."[3]

West's explanation of the meaning of these two passages and her view of homosexual relations as a political tool is based on the writings of Professor Mary Tolbert. She quotes Tolbert's paper, which was delivered at the Lancaster School of Theology in 2002, "Homoeroticism in the Biblical World: Biblical Texts in Historical Contexts."[4] Those who champion Christian homosexuality have difficulty dealing with the six texts in the Bible that treat this subject. Mary Tolbert's attempt to get around the three New Testament passages that condemn homosexual practice has been used by many GLBT theologians and constitutes a classic example of their manipulation of the biblical text.

Tolbert, who is the executive director of Pacific School of Religion's Center for Lesbian and Gay Studies in Religion and Ministry, is a very strong advocate for homosexual causes and an ardent defender of homosexuality as an alternative Christian lifestyle (even though she doesn't like the word *homosexuality*, preferring the term *homoeroticism*). I have read Tolbert's entire paper. It focuses on homoerotic relations recorded in selected literary fragments from various Mediterranean cultures, including Rome, Greece, Assyria and Egypt. After she compiles references to homoeroticism in these fragments, she concludes that both the Hebrew Bible and the New Testament reflect those views. If what Professor Tolbert affirms is to be taken as fact, she would have to prove (1) that what she describes as the political use of homosexual intercourse was the dominant view of homosexuality in the ancient Mediterranean region rather than just a collection of isolated proof texts for her lesbian perspective, and (2) that the authors of the Hebrew Bible and New Testament were not only influenced by those views but espoused them. In her paper, she has established neither of these. Her quotes are sporadic and marginal at best. Even more important, she makes no attempt to prove that the Hebrews or early Christians shared any of those views, precisely because there are absolutely no such indications in the Bible. The Old and New Testaments *never* equate same-sex relations with political dominance. That entire construction by Tolbert is a fanciful theory that she imposes on the biblical text to make it say what she wants it to say. This is one of the worst examples of what theologians call *eisegesis* I have ever seen! *Eisegesis* is defined as reading one's own opinions into the text instead of trying to see what the text is actually saying. Tolbert goes to great lengths to reinterpret the Bible through the lens of her understanding of homoeroticism, but she neither establishes her view as representative of the nations surrounding Israel nor does she provide evidence of its acceptance by the biblical authors. Though homosexual theologians go to great lengths to make their point, their reinterpretation of Scripture is on very shaky ground.

Suffice it to say that the two Leviticus passages are abundantly clear. In God's eyes homosexual relations are an abomination so serious that in Israel they should be punished by death. There is really no room for debate in these passages. The only way to get around them is to perform the kind of interpretive gymnastics (methods that enable the interpreter to avoid the clear meaning of the text) that Professor Tolbert and therefore Dr. West have practiced.

ROMANS 1

In Romans 1:26-27 Paul states that the end result of the pagan world's rejection of God is that he

> gave them over to degrading passions; for their women exchanged the natural function for that which is unnatural, and in the same way also the men abandoned the natural function of the woman and burned in their desire toward one another, men with men committing indecent acts and receiving in their own persons the due penalty of their error.

Here homosexuality, both feminine and masculine, is seen as the result of a rebellious rejection of God. It is described as "degrading passions," "unnatural," "indecent acts" and "error." In Scripture, God turns people over to their sins so that they can see the negative results and hopefully repent. This is exactly what he did to the Gentile sinners, and the sin of homosexuality was a part of those consequences.

For West "these verses must be read in the cultural context of the Mediterranean world that understood socially acceptable sexual behavior to happen only one way: among unequals with the dominant partner always an adult male."[5] However, this "dominance motif" is not found anywhere in the writings of Paul or anywhere in the entire New Testament.

These verses in Romans 1 constitute clear Christian teaching on homosexual conduct as a degrading, unnatural, indecent error. Paul goes on to say that those practices are the result of God giving "them over to a depraved mind" (Romans 1:28). The Greek word used for "depraved" here is *adokimos*, which means "corrupted." Homosexuality, which degrades people, is unnatural and indecent. It springs from a corrupted mind that does not recognize its own error. It is totally unacceptable for Christians.

FIRST CORINTHIANS 6 AND 1 TIMOTHY 1

Although Dr. West never refers to these two passages in her article, she has dealt with them when she has come to my class to speak to my students. (After her presentation, I shared the Bible's view on this subject.) In 1 Corinthians 6:9-10, Paul states that neither the "effeminate" (probably referring to male prostitutes) nor "homosexuals" will "inherit the kingdom of God." This passage is so straightforward that it has become a serious obstacle for the homosexual community. Paul goes on to say, "Such were some of you; but you were washed" (v. 11). This is the New Testament answer to the question, Can homosexuals be transformed into heterosexuals by God? The answer is a resounding yes!

Paul also points out in 1 Timothy 1:9-10 that the law is made "for those who are lawless and rebellious, for the ungodly and sinners, for the unholy and profane, for those who kill their fathers or mothers, for murderers and immoral men and homosexuals." Again, Paul makes it plain that homosexuals are included in this list of sinners and ungodly people. Homosexuality is not an acceptable alternative lifestyle; it is sin.

In her oral presentation, West suggested that these two passages do not refer to loving, caring same-sex relations but to male prostitution and abusive, ungodly same-sex relations. However, when I have evaluated her talks with my students the next class period, I have pointed out that neither passage leaves room for that interpretation. The practice of homosexuality is condemned as a sin, and those who practice it are excluded from the kingdom of God. Can it be any clearer than that?

Dr. West ends her paper with a brief discussion of "Issues of Biblical Authority." She insists that, "While the Bible is an important witness to the relationship between God and humanity, it is not the ultimate revelation of God—Jesus Christ, the Word made flesh, is." This idea, used by many modern theologians, seeks to erode confidence in the authority of God's Word for our lives. As usual, there is a reason for this strategy: avoiding the plain teaching of Scripture against things that people want to do. West has fallen into this unfortunate trap. To avoid the plain teaching of Scripture against homosexuality, she has chosen rather to question and undermine the authority of the Scriptures by claiming that they are not the real Word of God. This typical liberal ploy seeks to remove the sting of God's Word when it touches a nerve in our conduct.

We are all vulnerable to this conviction-avoiding trap, and we must all guard against it. The Word of God makes us uncomfortable. It convicts us of our sins and shows us how to escape them, but sometimes we don't want to escape. So we find ways to avoid what God's Word says in order to reduce that tension. Heterosexuals and homosexuals do this. Both groups must repent of this sin and submit our lives to the powerful, inspired Word of God.

A CHRISTIAN VIEW OF HOMOSEXUALITY

Christians need to make sure that our response to homosexuals is loving and kind. We know from God's Word that homosexuality is an unnatural and sinful act, but that does not give us license to abuse homosexuals in any way. We are all sinners, we all need Christ to save us, and we are all far from the Christian ideal of human conduct.

In our reaction to homosexuality we must keep in mind that

1. We are supposed to love everyone, regardless of their sin. This means no jokes, no hatred, no attacks, no contempt and no disdain for homosexuals. One of the most disturbing elements of this debate is the television broadcast of so-called Christians at gay pride pa-

rades carrying signs that say "Faggots, go to hell!" or "God hates homos!" This is not the spirit of Christ. It just adds fuel to the fire of those who think all Christians are homophobic and hateful. It is not worthy of the Lord who died for homosexuals too.

2. In a sense homosexuality is like any other sin. The New Testament condemns greed four times as much as it does homosexuality. Isn't it curious to see how loudly some Christians can condemn sins that do not tempt them, but how silent they are about sins like greed, pride and selfishness that attract them? However, it is important to remember that, in one sense, homosexuality is not like all other sins. It is one of the sins that can keep people out of heaven. Ultimately, this issue is not one of bad sins versus worse sins, but a question of repentance. All are sinners, but all are not unrepentant sinners. The man who looks at porn and lusts after a naked woman has committed a sin. But if he confesses to God that he has sinned, removes the porn from his computer and asks God to help him resist that temptation, he is a repentant sinner. Those who continue living in homosexual relationships are also sinners, but they are unrepentant, just like the Christian who continues to view porn even though he knows it is wrong. Yes, all are sinners, but all are not unrepentant sinners.

3. There is a difference between homosexual *attraction* and homosexual *behavior*. Homosexual attraction means that people are sexually attracted to individuals of the same gender. Homosexual behavior means that people act on their same-gender attraction and sexually engage people of the same gender. If, as a Christian, I am attracted to a beautiful woman even though I am married, I don't have to act on that attraction. In fact, I am truer to myself if I restrain myself than if I commit adultery. Just as we expect lustful heterosexuals to abstain from sex outside of marriage, so we also expect those with homosexual attraction to refrain from sexual activity outside of Christian marriage. We should accept those with homosexual *attraction* as full members of our churches if they commit themselves not to take part in homosexual *behavior*.

4. We should accept homosexuals into our churches just as we

accept all sinners—not to condone their sin but to love them and let Jesus transform their (and our) lives.

THE HOMOSEXUAL GENE

Going back to our original question, yes, according to the Word of God, homosexuality is a serious sin, not just an alternative lifestyle. The question about whether people are born homosexual, that is, made that way by God and therefore not responsible for their conduct, also needs to be addressed. It would be patently unjust for God to create a person homosexual and then condemn that person for it.

Nancy Wilson, current moderator of the Metropolitan Community Churches, has spoken in my classes several times. One day, a practicing lesbian asked her, "Are people born homosexual or is it something they learn?" I expected Wilson to say that homosexuals are born that way, but to my surprise, she answered that there is no scientific evidence that people are born homosexual. She added that she hoped that one day scientists will discover the existence of a "homosexual gene" or different brain configuration in homosexuals, but that so far that is not the case. Wilson would have much to gain by supporting the spurious Internet declarations about "the homosexual gene" and other possible genetic explanations of homosexuality, so the fact that she rejects them as false speaks volumes about that issue and about her personal integrity.

BEING TENDER WITH HOMOSEXUALS

Looking homosexual students in the eye and answering their question about whether or not homosexuality is a sin is one of the most painful things I have done. It hurts me to see the pain and rejection in their eyes as I try to lovingly share with them what I think God's Word says. I have many homosexual friends, and I love and respect them greatly. I know that when I talk to them about giving their lives to Christ, I am asking them to make a far greater sacrifice than I had to make to become a Christian. They are being asked to give up the person they love, to whom they have committed themselves, the person who accepts and loves them just as they are. That is rough. We need to be extremely kind and understanding as we relate to homosexuals. Many of them have been bashed, insulted and mistreated by Christians, and the sting of that does not go away easily. In the final analysis we all must give up our sins to come to Christ, and they too must come to see that salvation, joy, forgiveness, abundant life and eternity with God are more important than anything else. In spite of all the side issues in this debate, Paul's words are still wonderfully encouraging and hope-filled for homosexuals and for all of us: "Such were some of you; but you were washed, but you were sanctified, but you were justified in the name of the Lord Jesus Christ and in the Spirit of our God" (1 Corinthians 6:11). God can change all of us—even homosexuals—if we turn to him in faith and obedience.

PRAYING THE PRINCIPLE

Lord, I confess to you today that I have not always been faithful to you in my use of my body. Please forgive me and cleanse me from all sexual sin, and help me, Lord, to approach homosexuals with humility and vulnerability so that I can show them the freedom and deliverance that come from surrendering to you.

> Flee immorality. Every *other* sin that a man commits is outside the body, but the immoral man sins against his own body. Or do you not know that your body is a temple of the Holy Spirit who is in you, whom you have from God, and that you are not your own? For you have been bought with a price: therefore glorify God in your body. (1 Corinthians 6:18-20)

DISCUSSING THE PRINCIPLE

1. What were the two basic positions on homosexuality espoused by the author's students? Why was it so hard to keep discussions of this issue respectful and civil? Have you experienced that problem?

2. Identify the six biblical passages about homosexuality. What are

Dr. West's interpretations of their meaning, and the author's response to her interpretations? What is your view of these passages and the issue of homosexuality and Christianity?

3. Summarize the author's four final thoughts on how Christians should treat homosexuals. Do you agree with those suggestions?

4. Is there a homosexual gene? Defend your answer.

5. What factors do we need to keep in mind when dealing with homosexuals?

6. What is the biblical hope for homosexuals? Are you willing to share that hope with them in a loving, accepting, tender way?

Conclusion

We have covered a great deal of territory in this book. I hope it has been helpful. If you are not yet a believer, I hope this book has challenged you to consider the Christian faith seriously and that it has removed some of the mental obstacles to putting your trust in Christ. If you are a believer, I hope this book has deepened your understanding of the faith and strengthened your resolve to speak to others about the good news of Jesus Christ.

There are many more questions that need to be answered. If you would like to send me a question for consideration for a possible future volume, or to get updates about a second volume of this project with twenty-five more advanced questions and answers about the Christian faith, go to AskDoctorRay.net.

> Sanctify Christ as Lord in your hearts, always *being* ready to make a defense to everyone who asks you to give an account for the hope that is in you, yet with gentleness and reverence. (1 Peter 3:15)

Appendix

This appendix provides the opportunity to practice the principles of Bible study outlined in chapter 13, "What Is the Best Way to Study the Bible?"

THE EXAMPLE OF MARK 2

Let's hone our inductive Bible study skills using the narrative of Mark 2:1-12, which focuses on Jesus as the Son of Man. On the left side of the chart, I have summarized the verses and suggested the structural connections in them to give you a chance to fill in the details on the right-hand column.

Verse:	Structure:	Your comments:
vv. 1-2. Jesus returned to Capernaum and many gathered to hear him.	Cause-Effect	Cause: _____ Effect: _____
vv. 3-4. Four men brought a paralyzed man to see Jesus, but because of the crowd they couldn't get to Jesus, so they lowered their friend through the roof.	Cause-Effect	Cause: _____ Effect: _____

v. 5. Seeing their faith, Jesus said to the man, "Son, your sins are forgiven."	Cause-Effect	Cause: _____ Effect: _____
vv. 6-7. Some of the scribes wondered why Jesus said that—they thought he was blaspheming since only God can forgive sins.	Effect-Cause	Effect: _____ Cause: _____
v. 8. Jesus knew what they were thinking, so he said, "Why are you reasoning about these things in your hearts?"	Cause-Effect	Cause: _____ Effect: _____
vv. 9-11. Jesus asks them which is easier—to forgive sins or to heal a paralytic? Then, so they could know that Jesus has power to forgive sins, Jesus said to the paralytic, "Get up, pick up your pallet and go home."	Contrast with Means-Goal	Contrast: _____ _____ Means: _____ Goal: _____
v. 12. The man was healed, so the people were amazed and glorified God saying, "We have never seen anything like this."	Cause-Effect	Cause: _____ Effect: _____

What is the main message of this passage? How can you apply that message to your own life? Has Jesus done for you what he did for the paralyzed man, both forgiving and healing you? What is your response to what he has done for you? The answers to these questions will help you to apply the message of the passage to daily life. I pray God uses this exercise to whet your appetite for a lifetime of serious study of his Word!

For more help with this kind of Bible study, see Robert Traina, *Methodical Bible Study* (Grand Rapids: Zondervan, 1980); Gordon D. Fee and Douglas Stuart, *How to Read the Bible for All Its Worth*, 3rd ed. (Grand Rapids: Zondervan, 2003); or Kay Arthur, *How to Study Your Bible: The Lasting Rewards of the Inductive Method* (Eugene, OR: Harvest House, 2001).

Notes

Chapter 1: Why Would Anyone Believe the Bible Is the Inspired Word of God?

[1]Basil Mitchell, *The Justification of Religious Belief* (London: Macmillan, 1973).

[2]Peter Stoner and Robert C. Newman, *Science Speaks: Scientific Probability and Biblical Prophecy* (Chicago: Moody Press, 1976). This work, quoted by Josh McDowell in his *Evidence That Demands a Verdict* (San Bernardino: Campus Crusade, 1972), was revised and HTML formatted in 2005 by Stoner's grandson, Don W. Stoner, and is available online at www.sciencespeaks.net. It has never been mathematically refuted since the time of its publication.

[3]For further confirmation of the archaeological verification of biblical facts, see Joseph M. Holden and Norman Geisler, *The Popular Handbook of Archaeology and the Bible: Discoveries That Confirm the Reliability of Scripture* (Eugene, OR: Harvest House, 2013), and *Wycliffe Dictionary of Biblical Archaeology*, ed. Charles F. Pfeiffer (Peabody, MA: Hendrickson, 2000).

[4]The Dead Sea Scrolls are ancient documents dating from 400–300 B.C. and were found in Qumran, near the Dead Sea. They contain biblical texts and extrabiblical writings of the Essene community that produced them.

[5]M. H. Shakir, *Qur'an Translation* (Elmhurst, NY: Tahrike Tarsile Qur'an, 1999).

[6]"Project Combat Launched to Eradicate Devadasi System," *The Hindu*, January 30, 2006.

[7]Bob Wilkerson, "Testimonies: How Religious Scripture Has Changed My Life," *Helium*, January 10, 2008, www.helium.com/items/786445-testimonies-how-religious-scripture-has-changed-my-life.

Chapter 2: Isn't the Bible Full of Contradictions?

[1]If you would like to read more on this topic of contradictions in the Bible, I heartily suggest Norman Geisler and Thomas Howe's excellent book *The Big Book of Bible Difficulties: Clear and Concise Answers from Genesis to Revelation* (Grand Rapids: Baker, 1992), and Gleason L. Archer's equally helpful work *The New International Encyclopedia of Bible Difficulties* (Grand Rapids: Zondervan, 2001). They share with me the view that there are no real contradictions in Scripture.

Chapter 3: Why Were the Books of the Bible Accepted as Scripture, but Other Books Were Not?

[1]Elaine Pagels, *The Gnostic Gospels* (New York: Vintage Books, 1979), and *Beyond Belief: The Secret Gospel of Thomas* (New York: Random House, 2004). Karen L. King, *What Is Gnosticism?* (Cambridge, MA: Harvard University Press, 2003). Elaine Pagels and Karen L. King, *Reading Judas: The Gospel of Judas and the Shaping of Christianity* (New York: Viking Adult, 2007).

[2]José Míguez Bonino, *Doing Theology in a Revolutionary Situation* (Minneapolis: Fortress Press, 1975), pp. 86-87.

[3]Roland K. Harrison, *Introduction to the Old Testament* (Grand Rapids: Eerdmans, 1969), p. 268.

[4]Ibid.

[5]For example, church fathers such as Papias, Irenaeus and Clement and influential church leaders such as Tertullian, Origen and Jerome all confirmed that Mark was Peter's interpreter and that he wrote his Gospel under Peter's instructions.

[6]These apocryphal works were written in the third or fourth centuries, after the deaths of the last apostles; therefore they could not have come from the apostles.

Chapter 4: Can We Believe in the Biblical Account of the Resurrection of Jesus?

[1]G. B. Hardy, *Countdown: A Time to Choose* (Chicago: Moody Press, 1970), quoted in Josh McDowell, *Evidence That Demands a Verdict* (San Bernardino: Campus Crusade, 1972).

[2]I am indebted for some of this chapter's content to Josh McDowell and his outstanding book *Evidence That Demands a Verdict*. His influence on my thinking as a Christian has been incalculable. For further study on the truth of the resurrection, I strongly recommend William Lane Craig's exceptional book *Assessing the New Testament Evidence for the Historicity of the Resurrection of Jesus* (Lewiston, NY: Edwin Mellen, 1989).

Chapter 6: What Is Sin, and Why Is It Such a Big Deal to God?

[1]You can read more about the missionaries to the Huaorani in Elisabeth Elliot's book *Through Gates of Splendor* (Wheaton, IL: Tyndale House, 1986).

Chapter 7: Is Hell a Literal Place of Burning Torture, and Who Goes There?

[1]The term *Hades* is used in Luke 16:19-31 to describe a place of literal torment in which the condemned rich man begs the Father to "send Lazarus so that he may dip the tip of his finger in water and cool off my tongue, for I am in agony in this flame." Those who see hell as a spiritual rather than physical reality see this passage as merely a parable with symbolic language that should not be forced into a literal interpretation. But those who see hell as a physical reality suggest that this is not a parable, since Jesus actually names Lazarus, which

he does not do in parables. For them, this use of Hades does not lend itself to any spiritualizing interpretations.

Chapter 8: Why Did God Create Satan?

[1]Joyce Meyer, *Everyday Life Bible* (New York: FaithWords, 2006), p. 1107.

Chapter 9: Can We Understand the Trinity?

[1]Reginald Heber, "Holy, Holy, Holy," 1826.

Chapter 10: Will Everyone Be Saved in the End?

[1]Rob Bell, *Love Wins* (New York: HarperOne, 2012), p. viii.
[2]Ibid., pp. 1-2.
[3]Ibid., pp. 10-11.
[4]Ibid., pp. 42-47.
[5]Ibid., p. 62.
[6]Ibid., pp. 102-9.
[7]Ibid., pp. 107-8.
[8]Ibid., p. 109.
[9]Ibid., pp. 141-60.
[10]Ibid., pp. 154-58.
[11]Ibid., pp. 154-55.
[12]Ibid., p. 198.
[13]"What We Believe," Christian Universalist Association, www.christian universalist.org/about/beliefs.
[14]Ibid.

Chapter 13: What Is the Best Way to Study the Bible?

[1]If you would like to go deeper into inductive Bible study, I suggest that you read Robert Traina, *Methodical Bible Study* (Grand Rapids: Zondervan, 1980); Gordon D. Fee and Douglas Stuart, *How to Read the Bible for All Its Worth*, 3rd ed. (Grand Rapids: Zondervan, 2003); or Kay Arthur, *How to Study Your Bible: The Lasting Rewards of the Inductive Method* (Eugene, OR: Harvest House, 2001).

Chapter 18: Is Islam a Violent Religion?

[1]This information is based on Bruce Lincoln, *Holy Terrors* (Chicago: University of Chicago Press, 2003), pp. 93-98, and my own research in State Department documents.
[2]"True Meaning of Jihad," IslamVirtue, www.islamvirtue.com/2010/03/true -meaning-of-jihad.html.
[3]Lincoln, *Holy Terrors*, pp. 102-3.
[4]For a full presentation of the 9/11 attacks and their link to Islam, see my "Islam After September 11," in Warren Matthews, *World Religions*, ed. Raymond Hundley (Belmont, CA: Wadsworth Thompson, 2003), pp. 171-81.

Chapter 20: What's So Important About Jesus?

[1]C. S. Lewis, *Mere Christianity* (New York: HarperCollins, 2001), pp. 52-53.

Chapter 21: Do Science and the Bible Contradict Each Other?

[1]For further study of the issue of miracles, see C. S. Lewis, *Miracles* (New York: HarperCollins, 2009); and William Lane Craig, "The Problem of Miracles," Reasonable Faith, www.reasonablefaith.org/the-problem-of-miracles-a-historical-and-philosophical-perspective.

Chapter 22: Can a Christian Believe in Evolution?

[1]There are many problems inherent in the theory of evolution. For further study see Norman L. Geisler and Frank Turek, *I Don't Have Enough Faith to Be an Atheist* (Wheaton, IL: Crossway, 2004), chaps. 3-6; and Jonathan Wells, *Icons of Evolution* (Washington, DC: Regnery, 2002).

Chapter 24: What Does the Bible Teach About Abortion?

[1]"History," Care Net, www.care-net.org/aboutus/history.php.

Chapter 25: Is Homosexuality a Sin?

[1]Mona West, "The Bible and Homosexuality," Metropolitan Community Churches, mccchurch.org/download/theology/homosexuality/BibleandHomosexuality.pdf.

[2]Ibid.

[3]Ibid.

[4]Mary Tolbert, "Homoeroticism in the Biblical World: Biblical Texts in Historical Contexts," Pacific School of Religion, November 20, 2002, www.clgs.org/homoeroticism-biblical-world-biblical-texts-historical-contexts-0.

[5]West, "The Bible and Homosexuality."